WITHDRAWN

cooking with
johnny vee

cooking with
johnny vee

International Cuisine with a Modern Flair

John Vollertsen
Las Cosas Cooking School

Photography by Kitty Leaken

Gibbs Smith, Publisher
TO ENRICH AND INSPIRE HUMANKIND
Salt Lake City | Charleston | Santa Fe | Santa Barbara

**Vista Grande
Public Library**

T 112326

First Edition
12 11 10 09 08   5 4 3 2 1

Text © 2008 John Vollertsen
Photographs © 2008 Kitty Leaken

All rights reserved. No part of this book may be reproduced by any means whatsoever without written permission from the publisher, except brief portions quoted for purpose of review.

Published by
Gibbs Smith, Publisher
P.O. Box 667
Layton, Utah 84041
Orders: 1.800.835.4993
www.gibbs-smith.com

Designed by m:GraphicDesign
Photo styling by Kimberley Loughlin
Printed and bound in China

Library of Congress Cataloging-in-Publication Data
Vollertsen, Johnny.
   Cooking with Johnny Vee : international cuisine with a modern flair /
Johnny Vollertsen ; photographs by Kitty Leaken. — 1st ed.
      p. cm.
   ISBN-13: 978-1-4236-0155-5
   ISBN-10: 1-4236-0155-6
   1. Cookery, International. 2. Cookery, American—Southwestern style. I. Title.

TX725.A1V625 2008
641.59—dc22
                                    2007041999

Metric Conversion Chart

Liquid and Dry Measures

U.S.	Canadian	Australian
¼ teaspoon	1 mL	1 ml
½ teaspoon	2 mL	2 ml
1 teaspoon	5 mL	5 ml
1 tablespoon	15 mL	20 ml
¼ cup	50 mL	60 ml
⅓ cup	75 mL	80 ml
½ cup	125 mL	125 ml
⅔ cup	150 mL	170 ml
¾ cup	175 mL	190 ml
1 cup	250 mL	250 ml
1 quart	1 liter	1 litre

Temperature Conversion Chart

Fahrenheit	Celsius
250	120
275	140
300	150
325	160
350	180
375	190
400	200
425	220
450	230
475	240
500	260

contents

preface

earning to cook is a lifelong journey. The first time we swirl a spoon around in a bowl combining real (or imaginary!) ingredients and transform the mixture, a clock starts ticking. Perhaps it's simply water and dirt that we stir together to create our first mud pie. Or on Mother's Day morning we attempt to mimic Mom's knack for merging a few pantry items together in hopes that, just as she so effortlessly makes happen, pancakes somehow appear.

Whether they are edible or not, our first creations still receive that all-important first food review. It is always heralded as perfect and we are congratulated for our talent and skill in the kitchen. We are immediately hooked and our cooking life begins.

If encouraged, our curiosity about food can flourish into a career that can include a hit TV show, a line of cookware, and a complete portfolio of packaged foods with our picture on the label—sold coast to coast.

If thwarted, a lack of enthusiasm about food can sentence us to a life of "eating to live" instead of "living to eat."

When Julia Child first entered our living rooms on the television around 1963, it was enough to sit back and watch her wrestle with a duck or stuff a loin of veal. We were busy learning a mind-boggling collection of cooking terms like *bain-marie* and *bouquet garni* and such kitchen techniques as "larding" and "emulsifying."

Home cooks of today, however, take their cooking as seriously as does the professional chef. They read about food voraciously and are inspired to try new ethnic cuisines, seek exotic ingredients, and bone up on kitchen skills. Learning about cooking and the science around it is a new form of entertainment.

As our culinary world expands we are becoming food savvy. We understand the zing of lemongrass and the pucker of tamarind in Thai dishes. We yearn to know how to darken a roux for gumbo without burning it, how to expose the tender heart of an artichoke, and how to roast a chile to reveal its heat and flavor. So we turn to our televisions, computers, and cooking schools to continue the edible education.

I was born in suburban Rochester, New York, in 1955, and grew up in an era when most meals I remember from my youth started with some sort of canned Campbell's soup.

A happy childhood included weekends spent baking and cooking with my maternal grandmother. For this former Methodist minister's wife, cooking was a fun chore. Her attitude helped me associate food preparation with relaxed play.

Dad worked at Kodak and Mom stayed home and took care of us and cooked dinner nightly. It was amazing the variety of dishes that emerged from cans of cream of mushroom, cream of chicken, and cream of celery soup, as well as dried French onion soup packets.

My first love was music and theater. But my father discouraged me from going into the performing arts. "People," he said, "may not always attend the theater, but they will always want to eat." I had been a grill boy and

facing: Shrimp a-smokin'

soda jerk in the local Woolworth's coffee shop, so I put my dreams of stardom on hold and headed off to college to get a "respectable" degree.

After graduating from Cobleskill College in 1975 with a degree in restaurant management, I headed to New York City to pursue my original lifetime dream: to become an actor. There I joined the legions of other struggling would-be actors, not on the stages of New York's theaters, but slinging hash in some of the Big Apple's hottest restaurants. Very early on it occurred to me that rather than be an out-of-work actor who *had* to work in a restaurant while waiting to be discovered, I could claim the restaurant business as my chosen profession (and wait to be discovered).

Alas, Broadway never called, but a very interesting journey within the food world pushed the promise of bright lights and fame into the background. After eight years working in a variety of popular and famous NYC restaurants in both the kitchen and the dining room, including Soho's Greenstreet, Tribeca's Odeon, and Larry Forgione's milestone, An American Place, I headed Down Under to Australia. I was hired out of New York by a Sydney-based company in 1985 to open an American-style restaurant and cocktail bar, and this project led to what became a chain of six Southwest-themed restaurants called the Arizona Bar & Grill.

In between training the cooks in the subtleties of chiles and teaching the waitstaff how to line dance to "Achy Breaky Heart," I was responsible for developing and promoting the Southwest theme. For research I visited Santa Fe numerous times and immediately knew I would someday settle here. After completing one more "Arizona" location in Wellington, New Zealand, I made Santa Fe my home in 1993.

I didn't love it right away—after the big-city life of a beautiful cosmopolitan city, life in sleepy little Santa Fe was a shock. After three more extended stays back in Sydney, however, my career in New Mexico finally started to blossom. I realized that all my years in Australia, instilling the heart and soul of Southwest cooking into the minds of my staff, had prepared me for an exciting and satisfying next step in my career: teaching cooking.

A one-year stint as Cooking School Director for the Jane Butel Cooking School in Albuquerque led to my appreciation and knowledge of the unique place food holds in the history and culture of New Mexico.

Reflecting back to my years as a cook in New York, I had always felt stifled in the kitchen doing the manual labor for long hours at little pay. Now chefs were no longer the poor slobs in the kitchen with the dirty aprons, but the entertaining front men who roamed the dining room and waxed lyrical about their culinary creations. This is where I wanted to be. The spotlights have been traded for gas burners, and the applauding audience has been paired down to a group of curious cooks who want to understand the magic of cooking.

We still applaud at the end of each class; however, the students are not applauding for me but for themselves and the success of creating delicious new recipes.

As someone who teaches about food and creates recipes for a living, it was only natural that I start to write about food. I started by covering the local food scene in a statewide publication called *La Cocinita* and now write a regular food gossip column in *The Santa Fe New Mexican* called "Side Dish." The exciting, creative, and tumultuous Santa Fe restaurant world is my beat.

My friendships and camaraderie with our local chefs

allow me to get the inside story on what's happening in their creative heads. I invite them to the cooking school to share their view of cooking and teach us all, including me, new dishes, cuisines, and food styles.

I also have the pleasure of playing the role of food editor for *The Santa Fean* magazine, a national publication that captures and chronicles the essence of Santa Fe living. As I research stories and learn more about food and culture, I am inspired to create new classes to share my newfound knowledge with my students.

Las Cosas Cooking School started in March 1999 and is tucked away in the corner of a beautiful, well-stocked kitchen store, one mile off the historic Santa Fe Plaza. *Las Cosas* means "the things," and the store is packed with everything you will ever need to cook with. And I do mean *everything*.

The store has been at different locations with different owners for over thirty years. But it is with the current owners, Karen and Mike Walker, that it has flourished and become *the* source for serious cooks in Santa Fe. The Walkers had envisioned a cooking school with primarily demonstration-type classes and had already designed a beautiful kitchen when I came on board. My experience teaching restaurant staff how to cook with a hands-on approach inspired me to rethink the school and, with a little tweaking of equipment placement, we are able to accommodate up to fifteen students per class.

Our inaugural class featured guest chef and friend Eric DiStefano from my favorite Santa Fe restaurant, Geronimo. We truly broke in the kitchen that night with an elaborate menu that had our maiden-voyage students cooking for four hours before getting a bite. The harried

above: Well-fed students

but jovial DiStefano kept uttering under his breath to me, "Are we having fun yet?" Once the meal was completed and everyone relaxed, his question was answered. Everyone had fun and word got out.

Class topics come to me in many ways. Some of our classes are ingredient-driven, like "The Art of the Artichoke," which celebrates that versatile thistle, or "Luscious Lobster Cookery," which arms the home cook with the knack for choosing, chasing, and flavoring our favorite delicacy.

One morning at 8 a.m., as I prepared for a class, I happened to answer the phone at the store and a gentleman on the other end of the line inquired simply, "Do you carry oyster openers?" As an oyster lover I was impressed that someone should be thinking about them so early on a Saturday morning and I was happy to report that, yes, in fact we had three varieties of oyster openers to satisfy his urge. The next month I offered an Oyster Fest class in honor of that quest.

Kitchen techniques can inspire a class topic, such as overcoming your trepidation of pressure-cooking or deep-fat frying in our class "Batter Up." We include knife skills classes, food processor technique classes, and even bread machine success classes.

Ethnic cuisines play a very important role in our schedule; is there anyone who doesn't wish they could cook Thai at home? Some cuisines fail to fire the imagination; I had only a few students sign up for a Korean cooking class I called "The Kick of Kim Chi." Despite the small group, we still managed to unravel the mysteries of fabulous Korean BBQ and the fiery pickled cabbage that graces the plates of Korean cuisine. I find it satisfying to fire the imaginations of even three students at a time.

Cookbooks, too, inspire us all, and some classes centered on cookbooks introduce our students to chefs from around the world, from as far away as Australia and as close as Texas. One class I offered featured recipes from Jean George Vongerichten's first cookbook and got a mention in our local press. Unfortunately for me, the story insinuated that Jean George himself would be teaching the class; I did my best to speak with an accent but I think I was found out!

From the shelves of the Las Cosas store come more ideas for class topics. All the great covered casserole dishes from Le Creuset as well as a line of Chilean clay pots we offer gave me the impetus to teach "Comforting Covered Casseroles." The intriguing domed tagine by Le Creuset has inspired Moroccan topics. The convenience of the Camerons Stovetop Smoker has me pulling together classes on smoking four seasons a year. Even the collection of

above: Linda having fun with Chef Johnny Vee

small but handy kitchen tools for prepping garlic or lemons deserve a class to demonstrate their use.

I do believe that if you own one truly great knife and a good cutting board, you can cook with the skill and dexterity of a world-class chef, but so many new gadgets make cooking faster, easier, and in many ways more fun.

Our motto at the school from the beginning has been "We cook for fun." I challenge myself daily to make sure that the information I give out at the start of the class on ingredients, equipment, and technique never sounds too scholastic or wanders into the realm of SAT exams or an algebra lab. If I see students yawn or eyes glaze over, I quickly change gears and head to the stove and get cookin'. We finish our education over our prepared meal.

Our classes are 99 percent hands-on, where the students get to participate in the cooking. Classes are limited to fewer than fifteen, and the students work in teams to create the meal. The chapters in this book are laid out exactly as they are on our school schedule. Some of the menus would make a great complete meal, but realize, of course, that the collections of recipes in a topical class like "Luscious Lamb Cookery" would suggest that you choose one recipe from the list to build a meal around. I have made recommendations of other recipes to pair with the different dishes to round out a menu.

Use this book as a source for individual recipes (found easily by title in the index) or as a way to teach yourself about a variety of cooking topics and techniques. Consider inviting a group of family and friends to join in the fun and follow my tips on how to create a cooking class in your home.

Remember to keep your time in the kitchen entertaining and let your guests choose the degree of skill required to pull off the recipe. Include the kids and assign the non-cooks to bartending or cleanup tasks so no one feels left out.

If you visit Santa Fe, we would love to have you join us for a class. Our schedule is available online at www.lascosascooking.com, and you may register there as well. In November 2006 we launched a second cooking school in the historic Mesilla area of Las Cruces, New Mexico, at our brand-new second Las Cosas store. Now foodies from the southern part of our state and nearby El Paso, Texas, can get in on the fun too.

As an observer and commentator on the diverse culinary adventure my career has led me on, I look forward to continuing to explore the wonderful world of food and then share that adventure with my students and readers. I marvel daily on how much good food there is out beyond the horizon and past the memories of my youth in Campbell's soup country.

At the top of one of my first schedules from 1999 is the proclamation "And we're off!!!"

Crack open this book and get cooking!

—*John Vollertsen*
Santa Fe, New Mexico

the cooking school pantry

We are very lucky in Santa Fe to have a wealth of shopping options for the groceries we use in our classes. I don't like to teach a recipe that requires combing the planet for ingredients or equipment; I think it frustrates budding cooks—life is too busy now. If any ingredient that I discover is too hard to source, we bring it into our store inventory and sell it in the gourmet food section that is attached to our beautiful tabletop store, adjacent to the main kitchen store that is home to the cooking school.

We sell Dean and Deluca products, as they carry a huge portfolio of spices that boast even the most unusual seasonings, including zahtar and smoked Spanish paprika. Olive oils, salts, vinegars, dried chiles, and baking chocolate are displayed among our vast cookbook collection to ensure our students can easily obtain the ingredients we inspire them to use.

My favorite grocery store in Santa Fe is Kaune Foodtown, located right near the state capitol building. Small in size but mighty in gourmet ingredients, Kaune often has those hard-to-find foodstuffs, and its staff is always happy to bring in any item I use regularly that we can't stock in our store.

During the summer the Santa Fe Farmers Market offers a bounty of food necessities—plump green chiles for our New Mexico–themed classes, local goat cheese, greens, squash, tomatoes—all available at their peak perfection.

I do utilize our big Albertson's store for main ingredients; a successful shopper must also know how to budget food costs. I regularly tell my students that the generic store-brand version of an ingredient—canned tomatoes,

beans, frozen vegetables, mayonnaises, and mustards—are perfectly fine in certain recipes.

For the truly exotic items, the Internet can help you source ingredients from the farthest corners of the globe. I get a kick out of ordering authentic goodies online for ethnic classes like my Cuban topics. Also the special salmon I bring in from vitalchoice.com and dry-aged beef from greatwestcattle.com help home cooks get the best there is, delivered right to their door.

We host field trips to our farmers market and teach students how to plan a meal based on what's available rather than shop for a menu you have already laid out. Our trips to nearby Albuquerque and the giant Ta Lin World Market are popular excursions hosted by chef Mu Jing Lau from Mu Du Noodles, my favorite local Pan-Asian restaurant. Mu takes us through the aisles and aisles of world products and demystifies their use and origin.

I implore you to explore tiny ethnic groceries in your neighborhood and have fun playing with food. That's the joy I hope you find in cooking from this book. Here is a list of basic and exotic ingredients to get you started.

Spices

Asafetida

Ginger

Galangal—wrap and freeze

Chiles—wrap and freeze

Lemongrass—wrap and freeze

Kaffir Lime Leaves—wrap and freeze
Curry Leaves—wrap and freeze
Thai Mint
Thai Basil
Star Anise
Chinese Five-Spice Powder
Szechwan Pepper
Wasabi
Tamarind
Thai Curry Paste (red, green)
Zahtar

Oils
Peanut
Toasted Sesame
Vegetable
White Truffle

Vinegars
Balsamic
Cider
Red Wine
Sherry
White Wine
White
Rice
Mirin

Rice
Jasmine
Basmati

Sweet Sticky Rice
Black Sticky Rice
Sushi
Paella Rice—Bomba or Valencia

Flours
All-Purpose
Whole Wheat
Spelt
Rice
Sweet Potato
Chickpea

Noodles
Japanese Udon
Somen
Rice
Mung Bean

Wonton Wrappers
Spring Roll
Dumpling
Rice Paper

Vegetables
Baby Bok Choy
Shallots
Baby Corn
Shiitake Mushrooms
Oyster Mushrooms
Enoki Mushrooms

Sauces
Soy
Dark Soy
Fish (Thai—*Nam Pla*;
    Vietnamese—*Nuoc Mam*)
Oyster
Hoisin
Chili
Coconut Milk
Coconut Cream

*Great Gadgets**
Cameron's Stovetop Smoker
Garlic Press
Biscuit Cutters
E-Z Roll Garlic Peeler
Microplane Cheese Graters & Zesters
Bamboo Steamer
Rosle Mandoline
Mani-Kare Cut-Resistant Glove
Rick Bayless Pepper Roaster
Cuisinart Ice Cream Maker
Culinary Torch
Chocolate Rack

*All items available at
www.lascosascooking.com

acknowledgments

Cooking is such a cumulative skill; every person I have ever cooked with has taught me something. My grandmother Florence Chauncey started the education in her sunny upstairs kitchen in Rochester, New York.

The Wesley United Methodist Church that I grew up in hosted a weekly fish fry that I was lucky enough to help with, first as the operator of a big electric dishwasher and finally graduating to the important job of coleslaw and tartar sauce maker.

My first job as a busboy at a large Woolworth's coffee shop proved to be too menial for my young mind; I needed to wear the pointed paper hat and be the "chef."

Happily I moved up the ranks quickly and I have to thank my manager, Val Morrison, who encouraged me to pursue a career in hospitality. How lucky I was she saw in my awkward teenage enthusiasm for cooking the potential to go farther.

Hitting New York City as a green twenty-three-year-old was a frightening/exciting part of the growing process. My first touch with food fame came as a waiter at the groundbreaking "An American Place," Larry Forgione's tribute to classic American cuisine.

We rubbed shoulders with the likes of James Beard, Mimi Sheraton, Gail Green, Wolfgang Puck, and food critics from every major newspaper worldwide. Twenty years prior to the food channel's arrival, I saw what Chef Celebrity was all about.

Eight years in Sydney, Australia, taught me to appreciate what was special about America and our regional cooking. I managed a Cajun restaurant first called Jo-Jo Ivories, hot on the heels of Paul Prudhomme's fame, and then was involved in opening a small chain of southwestern restaurants called Arizona Bar & Grill.

One of my good buddies there was Über-chef Neil Perry, who has numerous restaurants, cooking shows, and cookbooks, and is designer of the menus on Qantas Airlines. Neil and his first wife shared an apartment with me for months while he was putting the finishing touches on his premier restaurant, Rockpool, which still flourishes today.

Upon returning to the USA, I spent a year as director of the Jane Butel Cooking School in Albuquerque, New Mexico. Jane versed me on the history of our indigenous cookery with her vast knowledge and love of this regional cuisine, details of which are featured in her many Southwest-themed cookbooks.

I especially have to thank Karen and Mike Walker, owners of the Las Cosas store. They have funded and supported the cooking school from the beginning, and we have thus far enjoyed a nine-year relationship of respect and success in both the store and the school. The Las Cosas staff, too, has helped promote our classes and registered our students, as well as kept me abreast of the areas of cooking our customers have expressed interest in learning about.

In November 2006 we launched a second cooking school in Las Cruces, New Mexico, at the new Las Cosas store located in historic Mesilla. How exciting it was to see the enthusiastic attitude and devotion to learn to cook from a whole new group of students. The fun continues!

Writing this book has also been a learning experience. Many of my recipes are developed to teach my students something new about an ingredient, cuisine, cooking technique, or equipment use. I wish to thank all my students who through the years have allowed me to use them as my guinea pigs to test and perfect the recipes you will now cook from this book.

My dear friends back in New York, the Adlers, were wonderful at testing recipes and sending me thorough notes from their testing. Barry and I cooked together years ago; though he is now doing corporate work, he is one of the most adventurous weekend home chefs I know. His wife, Suzy, gave me the "non-cook" perspective necessary in being able to engage even the most novice of cooks.

I must also thank Katharine Kagel of Café Pasqual's, who hired me to test recipes for her second cookbook and taught me the importance of detail and accuracy in recording recipes. It is through working with Katharine that I met photographer Kitty Leaken, who has brought my recipes and techniques to vibrant life with her keen eye and photographic genius. Kitty and I both get a kick out of the many photo ops that almost miraculously appear when I'm cooking and she's holding a camera.

And, finally, my many kitchen assistants, volunteers, and apprentices, who through the years have helped me organize, stock, and "work" the kitchen—I couldn't do it without you.

Each bite of food, each job I have had, each chef I have cooked with, each meal I have prepared, each friend who has encouraged me, all have nudged me along the path to this, my first cookbook. I have two hundred more recipes in my files yet to share with you, but let's get you cooking with these first.

above: Las Cosas Kitchen Shoppe & Cooking School, Santa Fe, New Mexico

fabulous
new year's brunch

NEW RECIPES FOR *AULD LANG SYNE*

– Menu –

- Eye-Opener Bloody Marys •
- Ham and Cheddar Scones •
- Cranberry-Ginger Scones •
- Sweet Crab Eggs Benedict •
- Berry Delicious Stuffed French Toast •
- Red Chile Cider-Glazed Potatoes with Bacon •
- Mocha Mint Tiramisu •
- Yogurt, Berry, and Granola Parfaits •

T o be fashionable nowadays, we must brunch," said the irreverent London weekly magazine *Punch,* way back in 1896. Brunch is that relaxed, mildly decadent meal that straddles breakfast and lunch—a dining concept devised for the benefit of people who have played too hard the night before. Brunch is my favorite meal. You don't have to get up early as it satisfies breakfast or lunch cravings. I have to have eggs before I can eat savory dishes, and the combination of eggs and hollandaise is a classic brunch pairing. It's a great way to entertain, especially if most of the preparation can be done the day before and then warmed and set out once you have woken up and joined the world of the living. Kick off the New Year with this festive menu. •

facing: Hollandaise on Sweet Crab Eggs Benedict

Eye-Opener Bloody Marys

This classic cocktail may have been named after Mary Tudor, eldest daughter of Henry VIII. She killed off many of her Protestant adversaries during her brief five-year reign as queen, which earned her the nickname "Bloody Mary."

Makes 1 pitcher

1 quart tomato juice, or V8, or Clamato

8 ounces vodka, or to taste

1 tablespoon Worcestershire, or to taste

2 tablespoons horseradish, or to taste

Juice of 1 lime

Tabasco or hot sauce, to taste

Salt and pepper, to taste

1. Mix all ingredients in a pitcher and serve over ice. Garnish with fresh celery sticks, lime wedges, and your creativity.

Chef Chat—
Provide a garnish bar and let your guests get creative with their own drink. Set out large stuffed olives, dill pickle spears, jalapeño peppers, baby corn, artichoke hearts, hearts of palm, pickled green beans, cold boiled shrimp, celery stalks, carrot sticks, lime wedges, cherry tomatoes, cucumber spears, mushroom buttons, and water chestnuts.

above: Chef Johnny Vee teaches

Ham and Cheddar Scones

Like biscuits and pie crust, scones benefit from not overworking the dough. As soon as the dough comes together you are ready to form them.

Makes 8 large or 16 small scones

2 cups all-purpose flour

2 teaspoons sugar

1/2 teaspoon salt

1 tablespoon baking powder

1/4 teaspoon smoked Spanish paprika

6 tablespoons unsalted butter, chilled

4 ounces Black Forest ham, diced

1 cup grated sharp Cheddar cheese, lightly packed

1 egg

2/3 cup milk, plus 2 tablespoons for glaze

1. Preheat oven to 400 degrees F (425 degrees F for high altitude).
2. Put dry ingredients in a food processor work bowl; pulse to blend.
3. Cut butter into small pieces and add to dry ingredients. Pulse until mixture resembles small grains of rice.
4. Transfer mixture to large mixing bowl, add ham and cheese, and toss ingredients together.
5. Whisk egg into milk in small mixing bowl. Add to flour mixture and stir until the dry ingredients are moistened and soft dough forms.
6. With lightly floured hands gather the dough together and press it out onto a baking sheet to form an 8-inch round.
7. Cut the round into 8 equal wedges and pull apart to separate them; place on the baking sheet.
8. Brush each scone with milk; bake until lightly browned and nearly doubled in size, about 18 to 20 minutes. Serve warm or at room temperature.

Cranberry-Ginger Scones

Yummy candied ginger, tart cranberries, and lemon zest . . . these scones are delish!

Makes 8 scones

2 1/4 cups all-purpose flour
1/2 cup granulated sugar
1 tablespoon baking powder
1/2 teaspoon salt
Zest of 1 lemon
12 tablespoons cold unsalted butter
2/3 cup finely chopped candied ginger
1/2 cup dried cranberries
3/4 cup cold heavy cream, plus extra for brushing
    tops of scones

1. Preheat the oven to 400 degrees F (425 degrees F at high altitude).
2. In a medium mixing bowl combine the flour, sugar, baking powder, and salt; stir to combine. Add the lemon zest and then, using a coarse grater, grate the butter into the bowl.
3. Toss the butter into the dry ingredients and then stir in the ginger and cranberries. Add the cream and stir the mixture until it forms a dough and all of the dry ingredients have been incorporated.
4. Turn the dough out onto a lightly floured work surface and gently knead a few times to gather it into a ball. Roll out dough on a lightly floured board to about 3/4 inch thick. Using a 3-inch biscuit cutter, cut out scones, cutting as closely together as possible.
5. Gather the scraps, pat and press the pieces back together, and cut out the remaining dough. Place the scones 1 inch apart on a baking sheet and brush the tops with the remaining cream.
6. Bake for 12 to 16 minutes, until they are slightly browned.

Sweet Crab Eggs Benedict

Anything with hollandaise on it is better! Remember, spinach makes this dish downright healthy.

Serves 4

1/4 cup butter, divided
4 cups baby spinach, washed and drained
Salt and freshly cracked pepper
1 cup fresh crabmeat
1 teaspoon sugar
2 tablespoons white vinegar
8 large eggs
4 English muffins, split, toasted, and buttered
1/2 cup Classic Hollandaise Sauce (see page 159)
2 teaspoons chopped chives

1. Melt 2 tablespoons butter in a large skillet. Add spinach and sauté over medium heat until the spinach has wilted. Season with salt and pepper, and set aside, keeping the spinach warm.
2. Melt remaining butter in medium saucepan and add crabmeat and sugar. Sauté until crabmeat is heated through and sugar is completely dissolved.
3. Fill a large deep saucepan with cold water. Add the vinegar, bring to a full boil, and then turn off the heat.
4. Carefully crack the eggs into the hot water. Turn heat to low and gently poach the eggs to desired doneness.
5. Meanwhile, top each half of the muffins with divided spinach and then crabmeat. Drain the eggs with a slotted spoon and place on top of crab. Ladle 1 tablespoon of hollandaise over each egg and garnish with cracked fresh black pepper and chives. Enjoy!

Chef Chat—
If your eggs and spinach have cooled off as you are assembling the dishes, pass each plate under a preheated broiler for one minute before garnishing.

facing: Poach, sauté, spoon, eat

Berry Delicious Stuffed French Toast

Here's a dressed-up French toast that holds well in a low oven and stays nice and moist.

Serves 4

3/4 cup whole-milk ricotta
2 tablespoons lemon juice
2 tablespoons confectioners' sugar
1 cup ripe berries (strawberries, raspberries, blueberries, or a mix), plus 1/2 cup for garnish
4 eggs
1 cup milk
1/2 cup heavy cream
2 teaspoons vanilla
1 teaspoon cinnamon
1/4 teaspoon nutmeg
Pinch cardamom
8 (2-inch-thick) slices brioche
1/4 cup butter
1 cup real maple syrup
1/2 cup vanilla or berry yogurt
Powdered sugar

1. Place ricotta in a fine mesh sieve and place over a medium bowl. Allow ricotta to drain for 30 minutes in the refrigerator. Discard the liquid that drains off.
2. Mix together ricotta, lemon juice, and sugar. Gently fold in berries and set aside.
3. Whisk together eggs, milk, cream, vanilla, cinnamon, nutmeg, and cardamom in a large bowl.
4. Using the tip of a sharp serrated knife, carefully slit open the sides of each piece of brioche to create a pocket. Using a small teaspoon, gently stuff the pockets with the berry-ricotta mixture.
5. Heat the butter in a large frying pan over medium heat. Dip each piece of bread in the egg mixture, coating both sides, and sauté until golden brown on both sides.
6. Place in preheated 350-degree-F oven for 10 minutes to warm through.
7. Serve French toast on warm plates with warmed maple syrup drizzled over it and 2 tablespoons of yogurt. Top with additional berries and powdered sugar.

Red Chile Cider-Glazed Potatoes with Bacon

In New Mexico we sprinkle red chile on everything we can. These potatoes are sweet and hot and delicious.

Serves 6

1 cup apple cider
6 large red potatoes
8 ounces bacon, cut into 1/2-inch pieces
2 tablespoons ground hot chile
1-1/2 teaspoons kosher salt
1 teaspoon freshly ground pepper
2 tablespoons chopped parsley

1. Place cider in small saucepan and simmer over medium heat until liquid has reduced to 1/4 cup. Remove from heat and set aside.
2. Wash potatoes and then cut each one into 6 pieces with a small paring knife.
3. In a large ovenproof roasting pan, sauté bacon just until it starts to become crisp. Add potatoes and allow to cook until potatoes start to brown.
4. Put potatoes in a 425-degree-F oven and roast until they are fork tender, about 15 minutes.
5. Remove potatoes from the oven and immediately pour cider syrup over them. Stir to coat evenly with cider and add chile, salt, and pepper. Garnish with parsley and serve while hot.

Mocha Mint Tiramisu

I love traditional tiramisu, but I played with the recipe to give it a holiday twist. Tiramisu means "pick me up" in Italian; but if you are serving this in the evening, it's a good idea to use decaf espresso to prevent keeping your guests up all night.

Serves 12

For the Zabaglione:
- 4 egg yolks
- 1/4 cup sugar
- 1/4 cup dry vermouth

For the Mocha Coffee:
- 1/2 cup espresso, chilled (decaf is fine)
- 2 tablespoons chocolate syrup
- 1 tablespoon sugar
- 1/4 cup rum

To Assemble:
- 72 ladyfingers
- Unsweetened cocoa
- Chocolate-covered coffee beans

For the Mascarpone Cream:
- 16 ounces mascarpone cheese
- 2 cups heavy cream, whipped with 6 tablespoons powdered sugar
- 3 tablespoons Peppermint Schnapps or white crème de menthe

Chef Chat—
A teaspoon of mint flavoring and a teaspoon of rum flavoring can be substituted for the alcohol in this recipe if you are serving it to kids. (The alcohol in the vermouth cooks out in the Zabaglione.)

1. Combine Zabaglione ingredients in a large stainless steel bowl over simmering water and whisk with a large balloon whisk until mixture thickens. Set aside to cool.
2. Fold together ingredients for the Mascarpone Cream in a medium bowl. Keep cold.
3. Combine Mocha Coffee ingredients in small bowl; stir to completely dissolve sugar.
4. Take a large casserole dish (13 x 9 x 2 inches) and spread a thin layer of Mascarpone Cream on bottom. Place a layer of ladyfingers into the cream.
5. With a pastry brush, soak ladyfingers liberally with Mocha Coffee.
6. Spread another layer of cream over ladyfinger layer. Dust with cocoa.
7. Repeat process until you use up ingredients: ladyfingers, coffee, cream, and cocoa, finishing with cocoa on the top. Garnish with chocolate-covered coffee beans.
8. Wrap in plastic wrap and refrigerate until ready to serve. (Overnight is best.)

Yogurt, Berry, and Granola Parfaits

There is a school of thought that the only thing that should be drinking milk is a calf! Goat milk yogurt is easier to digest than that made from cow's milk and has a nice extra tang. This is a festive and healthy start to a breakfast or brunch. I learned this recipe while working at the Vista Clara Spa and Ranch. It had been developed by the previous chefs, Steven and Kirsten Jarrett.

Serves 6

For the Granola:

1/4 cup thawed frozen apple juice concentrate
2 tablespoons real maple syrup
1 cup store-bought granola, any brand
2 cups old-fashioned rolled oats, uncooked
1/4 cup raisins

1/4 cup sesame seeds, lightly toasted
1/4 cup sliced almonds, lightly toasted
1/4 cup pecans, lightly toasted
1/4 cup flax seeds, lightly toasted

1. Warm apple juice concentrate in a small saucepan. Dissolve maple syrup in juice and set aside.
2. In a large, deep mixing bowl, combine remaining ingredients. Toss with a large spoon until completely mixed.
3. While tossing mixture, drizzle apple juice mixture over granola and mix well.
4. Scatter granola onto a large baking sheet and bake at 250 degrees F for 45 minutes or until granola is nicely browned and apple juice is completely evaporated. Cool and store in an airtight container.

For the Yogurt:

2 cups low-fat goat's milk yogurt, or any low-fat yogurt
2 tablespoons real maple syrup
2 tablespoons cold-pressed walnut oil

1. Whisk together all ingredients in a medium bowl and chill until ready to serve.

To Assemble:

6 large wine glasses
3 cups Granola (above)
2 cups Yogurt (above)
3 cups mixed fresh berries for garnish
Fresh mint for garnish (optional)

1. Spoon a quarter cup of granola into the bottom of each glass. Add three tablespoons of yogurt and then a quarter cup of berries. Repeat the layering one more time ending with berries. Garnish with more berries and sprigs of mint, and serve immediately.

comforting
covered casseroles

COOKED IN THE PERFECT POT

– Menu –

• French Onion Soup •

• Aussie Meat Pies •

• Real Flaky Pie Crust •

• Autumn Vegetable Pot Pies with Cheddar Cheese Crust •

• Moroccan Lamb, Fennel, and Date Tagine with Preserved Lemon Couscous •

• Quick French Cassoulet •

• Apple Rum Stew with Cheddar Cranberry Dumplings •

T his class was inspired by all the wonderful styles of cookware that can go on the stove and in the oven: Le Creuset, Chantal, All-Clad, and even the amazing micaceous clay pots created by master-potter Felipe Ortega. I love the idea of "one-dish cooking" for easy entertaining and cleanup. Some of these recipes can be made up in foil pans, frozen, and then thawed and baked at a later date—perfect for busy families. Nothing is more comforting than a hearty braised dish to chase away the cold weather months. •

facing: Chef Johnny Vee loves tagines

French Onion Soup

My first cooking job in New York City circa 1978 was at a cozy Eastside wine bar called The Wine Bistro. Every night we would prepare the onions for the morning cooks to finish and turn into this— our most popular soup. We left the onions in the oven overnight on 200 degrees F; the darker they get without burning, the yummier the soup.

Serves 6 to 8

2 pounds yellow onions

4 tablespoons butter

1 tablespoon flour

1 cup dry port or dry sherry

1 bouquet garni*

6 cups beef stock

Salt and pepper, to taste

1 baguette, sliced into 1/2-inch-thick rounds and toasted

2/3 cup grated Gruyère or Swiss cheese

1 tablespoon chopped parsley

A bouquet garni is 6 sprigs of parsley, 6 sprigs of thyme, and a bay leaf bundled together and tied in a piece of cheesecloth.

1. Peel and slice onions as thin as possible. Melt butter in the bottom of a heavy roasting pan. Add onions and stir. Sprinkle flour over onions and cover with aluminum foil.

2. Preheat oven to 300 degrees F. Place onions on middle rack in oven and allow to bake for up to 3 hours, stirring occasionally, until nicely browned.

3. Remove onions from roasting pan and deglaze pan with sherry or port over medium heat. Scrape onions into large soup pot. Add bouquet garni and beef stock.

4. Bring soup to a boil and turn down to simmer immediately.

5. Allow to simmer for 20 minutes. Season with salt and pepper. Discard bouquet garni.

6. Ladle soup into ovenproof bowls and top with toasted baguette. Divide cheese over baguette slices.

7. Place bowls under preheated broiler and grill until cheese is melted and bubbly. Top with chopped parsley and serve immediately.

Aussie Meat Pies

I lived for many years in Sydney, Australia, and learned to love this popular lunch and snack food. It's a throwback to the steak and kidney pies the Brits love and can be made in any size and served as an appetizer, lunch, or dinner main course. Try it with ground lamb, too, for a stunning difference.

Makes 2 (9-inch) pies or 3 (8-inch) pies

3 tablespoons butter

2 tablespoons vegetable oil, divided

1 pound mushrooms, diced in 1/2-inch cubes

1 cup diced carrots in 1/2-inch cubes

2 celery stalks, finely diced

3 garlic cloves, minced

1 medium onion, minced

2 shallots, minced

3 tablespoons cornstarch

2 pounds lean ground beef (under 15 percent fat)

1-1/2 cups beef stock

1 bay leaf

1 teaspoon fresh thyme

2 tablespoons Worcestershire sauce

1 teaspoon salt

1 teaspoon freshly ground pepper

1/4 cup minced parsley

2 recipes Real Flaky Pie Crust (page 19)

1 egg, beaten for egg wash

1. Melt the butter in a large heavy-bottomed skillet. Add 1 tablespoon vegetable oil and then mushrooms, carrots, celery, garlic, onion, and shallots. Sauté 4 minutes over medium heat. Sprinkle cornstarch over vegetables and stir to incorporate.

2. Remove cooked vegetables from skillet and set aside.

3. Turn heat up to high; add remaining vegetable oil and sauté beef until cooked through.

4. Add stock, bay leaf, thyme, Worcestershire sauce, salt, pepper, and sautéed vegetables. Stir mixture and turn heat down to a simmer.

5. Allow filling to cook until it thickens. Stir in minced parsley.

6. Roll out pastry and place in bottom of pie plates or tart shells. Remove bay leaf from filling and, with a slotted spoon, fill pastry shells. Roll out pastry tops and brush edge of bottom crust with egg wash. Lay top crust in place and crimp to seal. Cut 2 steam vents in top crust.

7. Brush tops with egg wash and bake at 375 degrees F until golden brown, 25 to 30 minutes.

Chef Chat—
The Aussies serve their meat pies warm with tomato sauce (ketchup) and mushy peas (mashed sweet peas). The peas are put onto a plate first, then the pie is set on the peas. This is lovingly referred to as a "floater." I discovered that they are a great hangover cure, as I'm sure the partying Aussies would agree.

Real Flaky Pie Crust

Our grandmothers knew the virtues of using lard to create the flakiest of pie crusts. Now that the deadly trans-fats have been removed from shortening, either fat will do.

Makes 1 (9-inch) crust

1-1/2 cups flour

2 tablespoons confectioners' sugar*

1/2 teaspoon kosher salt

1/2 cup very cold lard or non-trans-fat vegetable shortening

1 tablespoon chilled butter

1 egg yolk

1/2 teaspoon white vinegar

1/4 cup ice water

If using this crust for a savory dish, such as a potpie, leave out the sugar.

1. Place flour, sugar, and salt in a medium bowl. Cut the lard or shortening and butter into very small pieces and stir into the flour.

2. Using a pastry blender or two dinner knives, cut the fat into the dough until it resembles a coarse, dry, oatmeal-like texture. Stir in the yolk and vinegar and slowly add ice water, mixing until the dough comes together and easily forms a ball. You may not need all of the water.

3. Wrap the dough in plastic wrap and flatten it into a disc. Chill in the refrigerator for 30 minutes or until you are ready to use it.

4. Lightly flour a pastry board and roll the dough into an 11-inch circle. Form into pie plate and fill as per recipe directions.

Autumn Vegetable Pot Pies with Cheddar Cheese Crust

Why should chicken pot pie lovers have all the fun? This veggie version will satisfy even a hard-core carnivore.

Serves 6 to 8

Pot Pie Filling

3 tablespoons vegetable oil

1-1/2 cups chopped yellow onion

2 large garlic cloves, sliced

1 teaspoon fresh thyme

1 cup peeled and cubed pumpkin or butternut squash (1/2-inch cubes)

1 cup peeled and cubed baking potatoes (1/2-inch cubes)

1 cup peeled and cubed turnips (1/2-inch cubes)

1 cup peeled and cubed parsnips (1/2-inch cubes)

1-1/4 cups vegetable stock

Salt and pepper, to taste

1 tablespoon chopped fresh basil

1 egg, beaten for egg wash

1. In a large, heavy saucepan, warm the oil over medium heat. Add onion, garlic, and thyme, and cook for 4 minutes, stirring frequently.

2. Increase heat to medium-high and add cubed vegetables. Sauté until vegetables are slightly browned, about 6 minutes.

3. Add the stock, stir briefly, cover, and bring to a boil. Reduce the heat to medium-low and cook without disturbing for 6 minutes. Stir once, add salt and pepper, and cook until the vegetables are tender, about 6 minutes more.

4. Stir in the chopped basil and transfer to a deep pie dish or individual ramekins. Prepare Cheddar Cheese Crust (see page 21). Roll out to 1/4 inch thick on lightly floured board. Brush egg wash around the edge of a 9-inch pie plate or ramekins. Cover with Cheddar dough and crimp; cut 2 vents in top and brush with additional egg wash. Bake at 425 degrees F for 20 minutes or until crust is nicely browned. (Ramekins will take about 15 minutes.) Serve warm.

Cheddar Cheese Crust

2 cups flour

1/2 teaspoon garlic powder

1/4 teaspoon freshly ground black pepper

1/2 teaspoon salt

1/2 teaspoon smoked Spanish paprika

4 teaspoons baking powder

1/2 cup cold unsalted butter

1 cup shredded sharp white Cheddar cheese

1 cup heavy cream

Chef Chat—
One of my students excitedly reported that she used the Cheddar crust for the pastry in the Aussie Meat Pies and loved it.

1. In a medium bowl combine flour, garlic powder, pepper, salt, paprika, and baking powder.

2. Using a cheese grater, grate the butter over the dry ingredients and stir until mixture resembles coarse meal.

3. Stir in the cheese. Add cream and mix lightly with a wooden spoon until dough just holds together. Cover and let rest 10 minutes. Roll to desired thickness depending on use. Any extra dough can be cut into 1-1/2-inch-thick biscuits and baked for 10 to 12 minutes at 425 degrees F.

above left: Kitchen action

above right: It's all in the taste

Moroccan Lamb, Fennel, and Date Tagine with Preserved Lemon Couscous

This recipe is inspired by one included in the cookbook that comes with the Le Creuset tagine. I love the sweetness the dates impart to the dish but wanted it to be a bit spicy as well. Serve with my Preserved Lemon Couscous (see page 24).

Serves 4

3 tablespoons olive oil, divided

1 red onion, thinly sliced

1 fennel bulb, trimmed and thinly sliced

4 garlic cloves, thinly sliced

1-1/2 pounds lamb stew meat

3/4 teaspoon cayenne pepper

1 teaspoon ground ginger

2 teaspoons toasted and ground cumin seeds

2 teaspoons toasted and ground coriander seeds

Pinch allspice

1/2 teaspoon kosher salt

1 cup pitted chopped dates

2 cups chicken stock, divided

Cilantro sprigs

1. Heat 2 tablespoons of olive oil in a tagine and add onion, fennel, and garlic and sauté until the onions begin to brown. Transfer vegetables to a plate.
2. Add remaining oil to the tagine and add the lamb pieces; sauté until evenly browned.
3. Add all of the spices and salt to the meat, and cook for 1 minute over medium heat. Return the vegetables to the pan and add dates and 1 cup stock.
4. Cover and cook gently, stirring occasionally, until meat is very tender, 1-1/2 to 2 hours.
5. Add remaining stock, a little at a time, to keep the meat moist. Garnish with cilantro sprigs.

Chef Chat—
Lamb stew meat needs to cook slowly to become tender. Stews are ready once the meat has become fork tender. Of course, any good heavy casserole dish will do for this recipe. The domed shaped of the tagine creates steam that condenses on the dome and then runs back into the stew. This ensures optimum flavor from all those wonderful spices.

Preserved Lemon Couscous

Serves 6

3 cups vegetable stock

1/4 teaspoon ground cardamom

1/2 teaspoon red pepper flakes

3 tablespoons butter

2 cups couscous

1/2 cup preserved lemon, rinsed and then chopped
   in 1/4-inch pieces

2 tablespoons chopped cilantro

2 tablespoons chopped Italian parsley

Salt and pepper, to taste

1. Place the stock in a medium saucepan and bring to a boil. Remove from heat and stir in cardamom and red pepper flakes. Keep warm over low heat.

2. Melt butter in a medium casserole set over medium heat. Stir in couscous and cook for 1 minute, stirring constantly to coat with butter. Pour the stock over the couscous, stir to combine, and cover. Allow couscous to sit for 10 minutes.

3. Fluff couscous with a fork and gently fold in preserved lemon, cilantro, and parsley. Season with salt and pepper, and serve warm.

Chef Chat—
Preserved lemons are lemons that have been cured in a mixture of lemon juice and kosher salt. Sometimes spices are added such as cloves, cinnamon, bay leaf, coriander, and cardamom. Preserved lemons are easy to make but can be bought in many gourmet food stores and Middle Eastern markets. For a recipe, check out epicurious.com.

Quick French Cassoulet

The traditional version of this dish from the Languedoc region of France starts with dried beans and is cooked slowly all day. I created this quick version that is still yummy and takes a fraction of the time. The dish in which this is often baked is also called a cassoulet and is made of clay or porcelain.

Serves 6 to 8

2 tablespoons olive oil or goose fat (available canned in specialty food stores)

2 single chicken breasts, cut into 1-inch cubes

1 pound smoked sausage (Polish kielbasa), cut into 1/4-inch slices

2 confit of duck legs, shredded (optional)*

1 medium onion, chopped

2 garlic cloves, peeled and minced

1 can (14.5 ounces) peeled and chopped tomatoes

2 cans (15.5 ounces each) white beans

3/4 cup dry vermouth or dry white wine

1/2 cup chicken stock

1 teaspoon fresh thyme

2 tablespoons finely chopped fresh parsley

1/2 teaspoon freshly ground pepper

1/4 cup butter

1-1/2 cups dry breadcrumbs

Salt, to taste

Available mail order at www.markys.com

1. Heat olive oil or goose fat in bottom of heavy Dutch oven (I love the Le Creuset 5-quart Buffet Casserole) over medium heat. Add chicken pieces and sauté until nicely browned but not completely cooked. Remove chicken from pan and set aside.

2. Add sausage to Dutch oven and sauté until browned. If using confit of duck, add to pan and brown duck slightly.

3. Add onion and garlic to sausage, and sauté until onion softens, about 3 minutes.

4. Drain tomatoes and beans and add to pan. Stir in vermouth, stock, thyme, parsley, and pepper. Simmer over medium heat until liquid has reduced by one-third, about 10 minutes.

5. Meanwhile, melt butter in medium fry pan and add breadcrumbs. Stir crumbs until they are nicely browned.

6. Return chicken to Dutch oven, stir once, and season cassoulet with salt. Scatter breadcrumbs over cassoulet and bake in a 375-degree-F oven 30 minutes or until mixture is bubbling and baked through.

Apple Rum Stew with Cheddar Cranberry Dumplings

Serves 10 to 12

1/4 cup butter

1/2 teaspoon cinnamon

1/2 teaspoon nutmeg

1/4 teaspoon ground cloves

3 tablespoons real maple syrup

2 tablespoons brown sugar

2 tablespoons dark rum

8 medium apples, Granny Smith or other firm-fleshed apple

1. In a small saucepan, melt butter with spices, maple syrup, and brown sugar. When mixture is rapidly bubbling, turn off heat and stir in the rum.
2. Peel, core, and quarter the apples. Place in a large, deep, buttered casserole. Pour the butter mixture evenly over the apples. Cover casserole and bake for 20 minutes at 375 degrees F. Remove from oven and remove lid. Meanwhile, make the Cheddar Cranberry Dumplings.

Cheddar Cranberry Dumplings

2 cups flour

3/4 teaspoon salt

4 teaspoons baking powder

2 teaspoons sugar

1/2 cup cold unsalted butter

1 cup grated sharp Cheddar cheese

3/4 cup dried cranberries

1 cup heavy cream

1. In a medium bowl combine flour, salt, baking powder, and sugar.
2. Using a cheese grater, grate the butter over the dry ingredients and stir together until mixture resembles coarse meal.
3. Stir in cheese and cranberries. Add cream and mix lightly with a wooden spoon until dough just holds together. Cover and let rest 10 minutes.
4. Once you have removed baked apples from oven, use a large spoon and break off tablespoon-size dollops of dumpling dough. Drop onto the surface of apple stew.
5. Raise oven temperature to 425 degrees F and bake stew uncovered for 20 minutes or until dumplings are nicely browned. Serve warm with sweetened whipped cream.

Las Cosas
KITCHEN SHOPPE & COOKING SCHOOL
"LUSCIOUS LAMB COOKERY"

-Menu-

Rosemary Flatbread

Pecan Crusted Rack of L...

New Zealand Style L...

luscious
lamb cookery

AN AUSSIE FAVORITE

– Menu –

• Pecan-Crusted Rack of Lamb •

• New Zealand–Style Lamb Chops with Roasted Root Vegetables
and Homemade Mint Sauce •

• Luscious Lamb Osso Buco •

• Wild Mushroom Risotto with Truffle Oil •

• Yogurt and Zahtar Charred Lamb Riblets •

• Rosemary Flatbread •

Lamb is one of those wonderful meats that until recently was tricky to find in the market and considered a special-event dish or something you ordered in a restaurant. Now that it is more readily available, students are eager to learn how to prepare the many more-popular cuts. Having lived in Australia for eight years—definitely lamb country—I grew to appreciate how versatile an ingredient it is. Its pronounced flavor allows it to stand up to spices and seasonings. Look for organic cuts at the butcher and enjoy this delicious meat. •

facing: Recipes ready to cook

Pecan-Crusted Rack of Lamb

Serves 6

1 tablespoon olive oil

2 racks of lamb, 1 to 1-1/2 pounds each

Salt and pepper, for seasoning

1/4 cup Dijon mustard

1/2 cup finely chopped toasted pecans

1/2 cup plain breadcrumbs

1 teaspoon kosher salt, plus additional for seasoning meat

1 teaspoon freshly ground pepper, plus additional for seasoning meat

2 tablespoons lemon zest

1/4 cup capers, rinsed if salted

1 tablespoon chopped fresh thyme

1. Heat olive oil in large, heavy fry pan. When hot, add one rack of lamb, fat side down, and brown until some of the fat has been rendered. Remove from pan and set in roasting dish. Repeat with second rack.

2. Season racks with salt and pepper. Place racks fat side up and smear both with mustard.

3. In a medium bowl, combine remaining ingredients. Mix well and then pat mixture onto mustard-spread racks, pressing well to keep it in place.

4. Preheat oven to 450 degrees F. Place lamb into oven, crumbed side up, and immediately lower temperature to 400 degrees F. Bake for 20 to 25 minutes or until instant-read meat thermometer reads 135 degrees F for medium-rare, 140 degrees F for medium, or 165 degrees F for well-done. Allow rack to rest for 10 minutes before cutting into chops.

*facing: **Ready rack***

New Zealand–Style Lamb Chops with Roasted Root Vegetables and Homemade Mint Sauce

The Kiwis sure do love their lamb. NZ Lamb is appearing everywhere in the U.S. Shoulder chops are much more affordable than the racks.

Serves 8

8 lamb shoulder chops

Kosher salt

Freshly ground pepper

4 tablespoons olive oil, divided

4 tablespoons flour, divided

2 carrots, peeled and chopped

2 turnips, peeled and chopped

2 rutabagas, peeled and chopped

2 potatoes, peeled and chopped

1. Preheat oven to 400 degrees F. Place chops in a medium bowl and season with salt and pepper. Drizzle 2 tablespoons olive oil over the chops and toss to coat. Sprinkle 2 tablespoons flour over the chops and toss again.

2. Place root vegetables in a medium bowl and drizzle 2 tablespoons olive oil over them; toss to coat. Season vegetables with salt and pepper, sprinkle remaining 2 tablespoons of flour over them, and toss again.

3. Heat a large sauté pan and sear the lamb chops until they are lightly browned. Remove the chops and set aside. Turn heat to high and add root vegetables. Stir occasionally until they start to brown. Place browned chops over the vegetables and bake in preheated oven for 20 to 25 minutes, or until chops are cooked through. Serve with Homemade Mint Sauce.

Homemade Mint Sauce
Makes about 1/2 cup

1/4 cup cider vinegar
2 tablespoons sugar
1/4 cup chopped fresh mint

1. Combine all ingredients in a small glass bowl and allow to marinate 1 hour before serving.

Option for Mint Jelly

Reduce the amount of vinegar to 1 tablespoon. Place vinegar, sugar, and mint in a medium saucepan. Add 1-1/2 cups apple jelly and cook together until sugar is completely dissolved. Pour jelly through a strainer and chill to serve.

above: Mmmmint sauce

Luscious Lamb Osso Buco

Italian for "bone in the hole," Osso Buco is traditionally made with veal shanks. I think lamb has so much more flavor.

Serves 6

3 tablespoons olive oil

6 lamb shanks, approximately 10 ounces each

Salt and pepper, to season

1/4 cup flour

4 garlic cloves, minced

1 large yellow onion, diced

1 cup quartered mushrooms

2 tablespoons fresh thyme

2 cups chopped tomatoes

4 cups beef stock

1 cup dry red wine

1 teaspoon kosher salt

1 teaspoon freshly ground pepper

1 bay leaf

1. Place olive oil in heavy-bottomed Dutch oven or roasting pan. Season shanks with salt and pepper and dust with flour. Brown shanks on all sides in olive oil over medium heat. Remove shanks from pan and set aside.

2. Turn up heat to medium-high and add garlic, onion, and mushrooms. Sauté until onion starts to brown.

3. Return shanks to pan and add thyme, tomatoes, stock, and wine. Allow liquid to come to a boil. Add salt, pepper, and bay leaf.

4. Cover pan and place in preheated 400-degree-F oven and cook for 2 1/2 hours. Osso Buco is done when shanks are very tender and almost falling off the bone.

> *Chef Chat—*
> *Check the meat after 2 hours; you don't want the lamb to completely fall off the bone but to pull away easily. Serve with mashed potatoes or Wild Mushroom Risotto (page 36). Serve the shank with the wonderful rich gravy it produces over the starch dish. Osso Buco is a great dish to make for entertaining. You can cook it completely and then rewarm when ready to serve.*

facing: Stocking up!

Wild Mushroom Risotto with Truffle Oil

This creamy rice is perfect for catching all the luscious gravy the Osso Buco makes.

Serves 6

5 cups beef stock or mushroom broth

4 tablespoons butter, divided

2 teaspoons olive oil

1 tablespoon finely chopped onion

2 cups Arborio rice

3 ounces mixed dried mushrooms, reconstituted in
   1 cup water

2/3 cup grated Parmigiano-Reggiano cheese

Salt and freshly ground pepper, to taste

1 tablespoon finely minced parsley

Drizzle of truffle oil (available in gourmet food stores)

Parmesan shavings for garnish

1. Bring the stock to a slow simmer in medium pot. Strain mushrooms, reserving the liquid.

2. Melt 2 tablespoons butter and olive oil together in a heavy-bottomed pot and sauté onion until translucent. Add rice and stir quickly to coat the grains well.

3. Add 1/2 cup of warm stock to the rice and stir continuously until the liquid is gone. Add another 1/2 cup stock and repeat, allowing liquid to be absorbed before adding more stock.

4. Toward the end of the cooking, add the mushroom water in 1/2 cup measures. Continue adding stock until rice is tender but firm to the bite. Stir in reconstituted mushrooms.

5. Remove risotto from heat and add Parmigiano-Reggiano and remaining 2 tablespoons butter; stir until cheese melts and risotto is creamy. Season with salt and pepper, and stir in parsley. Transfer to warmed serving platter and drizzle with truffle oil. Top with Parmesan shavings.

Yogurt and Zahtar Charred Lamb Riblets

Yogurt is a great tenderizer and flavor enhancer. The zahtar adds a lovely fragrant kick of exotic spice.

Serves 6

2-1/2 pounds lamb riblets, or 18 small lamb chops

1 teaspoon kosher salt

1 teaspoon freshly ground pepper

2 tablespoons olive oil

6 garlic cloves, minced

1 cup plain whole-milk yogurt

Juice of 2 lemons

1/3 cup zahtar*

1/4 cup fresh cilantro

*Zahtar, sometimes spelled zaatar, is a North African spice mix comprised of toasted sesame seeds, sumac (edible of course), and dried thyme. Available from Middle Eastern markets and even Dean & Deluca spices, zahtar is great sprinkled over yogurt with pita bread for dipping.

1. Season lamb riblets or chops with salt and pepper. Place chops in a large bowl and drizzle with olive oil. Add garlic and rub to completely cover. Stir together yogurt and lemon juice in a small bowl. Cover lamb with yogurt mixture.
2. Sprinkle zahtar over lamb and coat both sides of riblets. Cover and refrigerate for at least 2 hours or up to 8 hours.
3. Prepare grill and cook lamb over direct heat until cooked to desired temperature.
4. Garnish chops with fresh cilantro.

Chef Chat—
Lamb riblets are smaller chops cut from the end of the rack. They are generally cheaper than the loin rack chops but just as tasty. Ask your butcher if he can save you some.

Rosemary Flatbread

My favorite cooking instructor, cookbook author, and restaurateur, James Campbell Caruso, gave me this recipe, which I have adapted. When visiting Santa Fe, don't miss a stop at his wonderful restaurant, La Boca, right downtown on Marcy Street. These fragrant breads go well with lamb dishes.

Makes 12 (6-inch) breads

4 cups flour

2 teaspoons baking powder

1 teaspoon kosher salt

1 tablespoon finely chopped fresh rosemary

2 cups plain yogurt

1 tablespoon olive oil

2 tablespoons roasted garlic, mashed with 2 tablespoons olive oil*

Extra olive oil for spreading

Kosher salt

1. Mix dry ingredients, including rosemary, in a large bowl. Stir in yogurt and olive oil. Knead until dough is smooth. Cover dough with a damp cloth and allow to rise for 1 hour (or half hour at altitude over 3,500 feet).

2. Cut dough into 12 pieces and roll each piece into a ball. On a lightly floured board, roll each ball into a 6-inch circle. Heat a cast-iron skillet and brush skillet with additional olive oil.

3. Cooking one flatbread at a time, cook 2 minutes on one side and then flip and cook 2 minutes on other side. Bread should puff and have nice browned spots on it.

4. Brush finished bread with roasted garlic and oil and sprinkle lightly with a pinch kosher salt.

   Alternatively, grill each flatbread over high heat about 2 minutes on each side or until flatbread is nicely browned and bubbled up. Remove from grill and finish as above.

*To roast garlic, take a whole head of garlic and turn it on its side. Using a sharp knife, cut off tip of the head 1/4 inch down, exposing the cloves inside the head. Drizzle olive oil over the cloves and sprinkle with kosher salt and freshly ground black pepper. Place head in a small ovenproof dish and add a quarter inch of water to the dish. Cover with foil and bake in preheated 400-degree-F oven for 45 minutes or until cloves are nicely browned and tender. Allow head to cool and then simply squeeze the head and cloves will pop out. Add olive oil and mash with a fork.

celebrating salty

COOKING WITH CAPERS, OLIVES, AND ANCHOVIES

– Menu –

• Olive Tapenade • Garden Herb Focaccia with Olives •

• Roasted Peppers and Potatoes with Bagna Cauda •

• Classic Caesar Salad • Chicken Piccata •

• Linguini Puttanesca • Sweet Fennel and Olive Mash •

• Olive Oil Cake with Lavender-Orange Syrup •

I often joke that I keep a salt lick next to the bed, so it only seemed natural to create a class that celebrates all those great foods with a salty kick. Salt is very important in the diet, helping to regulate the fluid balance in the body. Did you know that the presence of salt on the taste buds causes them to "pop-up," which increases the surface area of those taste-sensitive little cells, therefore increasing the ability of the tongue to register flavor?

Through the ages this valued commodity has been used as a method of exchange. Roman soldiers received a salt allowance as part of their pay. We have to agree how dull eating would be without it!

With the introduction of a wide variety of gourmet salts to the marketplace—exotic sea salts, smoked, Hawaiian sea, Himalayan pink, fleur de sel, and grey—suddenly an ingredient we took for granted has challenged chefs to be creative with it. My favorite salt, Maldon, is from England and has a light, flaky texture that makes it perfect for finishing a dish. Tossed onto grilled meats, it doesn't completely dissolve and adds salt and crunch to each juicy bite.

I'll take my salt any way I can get it: in capers, anchovies, olives, and the variety of dishes that feature them. Drink lots of water and enjoy these recipes. •

---

facing: Salty spread—olive tapenade

Olive Tapenade

If you're an olive fan, you know that tapenade is a heady, salty spread that's great on toasted baguettes, grilled fish, and chicken.

Makes about 2 cups

1/4 cup olive oil

2 tablespoons capers, rinsed

3 garlic cloves, chopped

6 anchovies

1 tablespoon Dijon mustard

1 teaspoon chopped parsley

1/2 teaspoon fresh thyme

1 teaspoon red wine vinegar

1 tablespoon brandy

1 1/2 cups rinsed, pitted, and chopped Kalamata olives

1. Place all ingredients except the olives in a food processor bowl fitted with a steel blade. Pulse a few times.

2. Add the olives and process again until olives are almost completely puréed but a little texture remains.

3. Cover tightly and store in refrigerator for up to 2 weeks.

above: Olive placement on focaccia

Garden Herb Focaccia with Olives

This is an easy bread dough that can also be used for pizza crust. Try it with fresh herbs or with the olives of your choice pressed into the dough.

Serves 6

2 teaspoons dry yeast

1 teaspoon sugar

1/4 cup warm water

1 tablespoon kosher or sea salt

1 cup hot water

3 1/2 cups flour

3 tablespoons extra virgin olive oil

1/2 cup whole pitted olives, or 2 tablespoons chopped fresh herbs
   (rosemary, oregano, basil)

1 tablespoon kosher salt for top

1/2 teaspoon red pepper flakes

Freshly ground black pepper

1. In a small bowl, dissolve yeast and sugar in warm water; allow to sit for 10 minutes. If yeast mixture does not foam, discard and start again with a new batch of yeast.

2. In a separate bowl, dissolve 1 tablespoon kosher salt in hot water.

3. In a medium bowl, combine yeast mixture, flour, and olive oil. Add salted hot water and mix to combine and form a fairly firm dough.

4. Turn dough onto a lightly floured board and knead until the dough is no longer sticky and is smooth and cohesive, about 8 minutes.

5. Place dough in lightly oiled bowl, cover with damp cloth, and allow to proof in a warm place until doubled in bulk, about 30 minutes.

6. Punch down dough and knead for 1 minute. Roll out dough and form an oval shape about 6 x 9 x 1-inch thick. Cover and allow to rise 20 minutes.

7. With oiled fingers, create fingers holes over surface of dough. Rub with additional olive oil and top with olives or herbs, remaining salt, red pepper flakes, and ground pepper.

8. Bake in a preheated 400-degree-F oven for about 18 minutes or until crust is crisp and browned.

Chef Chat—
This recipe lends itself to a variety of toppings: sun-dried tomatoes, anchovies, fresh mozzarella, whole pitted olives, caramelized onions. Be creative. I use my microwave to proof the dough. Bring two cups of water to a boil in the microwave. Place dough in microwave, leaving the water in there as well to create a nice warm place for the dough to rise.

Roasted Peppers and Potatoes with Bagna Cauda

I received an e-mail from a student asking if I had ever heard of this delicious warm vegetable dip from the Piedmont region of Italy. When I researched the simple ingredients, I knew it belonged on our Celebrate Salty menu. The name comes from bagno caldo, *Italian for "hot bath" . . . dive in!*

Serves 8 to 10

Roasted Peppers and Potatoes

1 1/2 pounds baking potatoes

2 tablespoons olive oil

2 teaspoons kosher salt

1 teaspoon freshly ground black pepper

2 large yellow bell peppers

2 large red bell peppers

1. Peel potatoes and cut crosswise into 1/4-inch-thick slices. In a shallow baking pan, toss potatoes with oil, salt, and pepper, and spread in 1 layer in pan.

2. Roast potatoes in a preheated 450-degree-F oven, stirring occasionally, until they are golden brown and slightly crispy, about 30 minutes.

3. Roast the peppers directly over a gas burner or under a broiler set on high heat. Turn peppers occasionally until skins are blistered and charred. Transfer peppers to a bowl and cover with plastic wrap; let steam, covered, until cool. Peel peppers and discard stems and seeds. Slice into finger-wide strips and set aside.

Bagna Cauda

4 large garlic cloves, chopped

1 teaspoon kosher or sea salt

5 anchovy fillets, chopped

1/3 cup olive oil

2 tablespoons chopped fresh parsley leaves

1 tablespoon chopped fresh oregano leaves

1. Mash garlic, salt, and anchovies with a mortar and pestle until a smooth paste forms. In a small saucepan, heat oil and garlic-anchovy paste over moderate heat, stirring, until it starts to bubble. Stir in parsley and oregano.

2. In a large bowl, toss peppers and potatoes with warm Bagna Cauda to coat, and season with salt and pepper. Arrange on a large platter and serve immediately. Make sure to have crusty bread on hand to gobble up all that salty oil left in the bottom of the serving dish!

Classic Caesar Salad

I love those Italian restaurants where the waiters prepare this popular salad tableside. Mixing the dressing in the bowl first is a throwback to that idea.

Serves 6 to 8

1 egg yolk*

1 tablespoon Dijon mustard

1 teaspoon Worcestershire sauce

2 large garlic cloves,** peeled and roughly chopped

3 tablespoons olive oil

6 anchovies, minced, or to taste

Juice of 2 lemons

1 head romaine lettuce

1 teaspoon salt

1 teaspoon freshly ground pepper

1/2 cup shaved Parmigiano-Reggiano cheese***

3/4 cup Toasted Garlic Croutons (page 47)

Additional anchovies for garnish (optional)

1. In a large bowl whisk egg yolk, mustard, and Worcestershire sauce together.
2. Add garlic, olive oil, anchovies, and lemon juice; mix well.
3. Separate lettuce leaves, wash, and pat or spin dry. Tear leaves into bite-size pieces.
4. Toss lettuce in bowl with dressing and season with salt and pepper.
5. Divide salad on chilled serving plates and garnish with shaved cheese and croutons. Top with additional whole anchovies if desired.

* If salmonella is prevalent in your area you can easily substitute 1 tablespoon mayonnaise for the raw egg yolk.
** The E-Z Roll Garlic Peeler by Harold Imports makes peeling garlic a breeze.
*** Gadget Gab—The microplane cheese grater turns hard cheese into soft shavings.

facing: Caesar stuff

Toasted Garlic Croutons

    1/2 loaf (1 pound) baguette

    2 tablespoons butter

    1 tablespoon olive oil

    2 garlic cloves, minced

    1/4 teaspoon salt

    Freshly ground black pepper

1. Tear bread into bite-size pieces approximately 1/2 x 1/2 inch. Melt butter in large sauté pan and add olive oil and garlic.
2. Over medium heat, sauté the garlic until it just starts to brown; add bread pieces immediately.
3. Sauté until the croutons start to brown. Season with salt and pepper and place on a baking sheet.
4. Bake in a 350-degree-F oven until croutons are crisp, about 10 minutes.
5. Croutons may be stored in an airtight container for 3 days, but allow them to cool completely before covering.

Chicken Piccata

Another classic Italian dish, this tender scallopine celebrates the pucker of lemon and the zip of capers.

Serves 6

3 large boneless, skinless chicken breasts, about 2 pounds total

1/3 cup flour

2 eggs

3 tablespoons unsalted butter

3 tablespoons olive oil

Salt and pepper, to taste

2 tablespoons minced shallots

Juice of 2 lemons

3 tablespoons capers

1/4 cup chopped parsley

1. Trim chicken breasts to remove any fat, gristle, or connective tissue, and slice each of them across the grain at a 45-degree angle into 6 1/4-inch slices. You should now have 18 slices of chicken. Pound each slice with the smooth side of a meat mallet until very thin, about 1/8 inch thick.
2. Put flour on a large plate. Beat eggs in a large shallow bowl.
3. Heat butter and olive oil in a large skillet over medium heat.*
4. Salt and pepper each chicken piece, lightly flour, and then pass through egg mixture and drain briefly.
5. Add chicken to skillet and sauté 2 minutes on each side, in batches, so that chicken lays flat in the pan. Place cooked chicken on large plate and set aside.
6. Turn up heat under skillet to high, add shallots, and allow to brown slightly. Add lemon juice and capers. Swirl the pan and allow juice to reduce by one-half; then add parsley and return chicken to pan. Stir to coat with sauce. Season with salt and pepper and serve on warm plates.

Chef Chat—
Covering each slice with a large ziplock baggie before you pound it will make this job easier.

Using both butter and olive oil to sauté gives you more time to brown meats before the butter starts to brown.

facing: Sautéing

Linguini Puttanesca

What could be more salty and tasty than this classic Italian sauce supposedly brought back to America by soldiers who were stationed in that country during World War II? I call this dish sexy.

Serves 6

1/4 cup olive oil

6 garlic cloves, sliced

1 can (14.5 ounces) good quality diced tomatoes

1/2 cup pitted black olives

1/3 cup capers, drained

6 anchovies, chopped

1/2 teaspoon red pepper flakes, or to taste

1/2 teaspoon freshly ground pepper

8 large leaves fresh basil, cut into chiffonade

1 pound linguini

1/2 cup grated Parmigiano-Reggiano cheese

1. Heat olive oil in a medium saucepan over medium heat. Add garlic and sauté until it starts to brown.
2. Add tomatoes with their liquid, olives, capers, and anchovies, and stir to combine. Reduce heat to low and allow sauce to simmer for 15 minutes. Stir in red pepper flakes, pepper, and basil, and remove from heat.
3. Cook linguini in a large pot of salted* boiling water until al dente. Drain noodles but do not rinse.
4. Toss pasta with the sauce and pile onto warm dinner plates. Top each serving with cheese and serve immediately.

Your pasta water should be as salty as the Mediterranean Sea.

Chef Chat—
Never rinse pasta noodles; it washes away the starch that the sauce should adhere to. Some Italian chefs even add a bit of the pasta water to the sauce to complete it.

Sweet Fennel and Olive Mash

Serves 6

3 large russet potatoes, peeled and chopped

2 tablespoons butter

1 fennel bulb, cored and finely sliced

1 large garlic clove

1/4 cup plus 2 tablespoons vegetable stock

1 teaspoon sugar

1 cup (approximately) heavy cream, heated

1/4 cup sliced black olives

Salt and white pepper, to taste

1. Cover potatoes with cold water in a medium saucepan and cook, covered, until very tender. Drain and set aside.

2. Melt butter in a heavy skillet; add fennel and sauté until fennel is nicely browned.

3. Add garlic to fennel and allow to brown slightly. Remove garlic and set aside.

4. Add 1/4 cup vegetable stock and cook over very low heat until fennel is tender, about 20 minutes.

5. Add remaining stock and sugar, and sauté fennel until it caramelizes.

6. Add reserved garlic clove to potatoes and pass both ingredients through a ricer.

7. Gently fold in enough hot cream to make moist mashed potatoes and then fold in fennel and olives. Season with salt and pepper, cover, and keep warm until ready to serve.

Chef Chat—
The more you mash those potatoes the more you develop the starch in them. Try using an old-fashioned ricer and then gently fold in the cream. Your potatoes will be light and fluffy, not like tile grouting.

above: Slow-braised fennel

Olive Oil Cake with Lavender-Orange Syrup

The wonderful flavor of lavender adds an exotic touch to this moist no-butter cake. Its light texture makes it perfect for breakfast as well as dessert when garnished with slightly sweetened crème fraîche. You'll love the strips of candied orange peel we reserve from the syrup to top the cake.

Serves 6

2 eggs

1/2 cup plus 3/4 cup sugar

Zest of 1 lemon

1/4 teaspoon salt

1/3 cup sweet Marsala*

1/3 cup milk

1/2 cup vegetable oil

1/4 cup extra virgin olive oil, plus extra to oil pan

1 tablespoon baking powder

1 1/2 cups flour

3/4 cup water

Peel of 1 orange, cut into 1/2-inch strips

2 teaspoons lavender, or to taste

1. Beat eggs and 1/2 cup sugar until they become lemony yellow.
2. Add lemon zest, salt, Marsala, milk, vegetable oil, and olive oil. Mix to combine.
3. Stir baking powder into flour and add to other ingredients, mixing thoroughly.
4. Smear inside of a 2 1/4-quart Bundt pan with olive oil. Pour in batter and bake in preheated 400-degree-F oven for 25 minutes or until cake is nicely browned.
5. Meanwhile, place remaining 3/4 cup sugar, water, and orange peel in a small saucepan. Make a lavender "tea bag" by placing lavender in a 4-inch-square piece of cheesecloth gathered and tied tightly with kitchen twine. Bring syrup to a boil and place lavender sachet in syrup. Allow to simmer until sugar is completely dissolved and syrup thickens slightly, about 15 minutes.
6. Discard lavender and reserve orange peel for garnish. Allow cake to cool for 10 minutes and invert pan on serving plate. With a toothpick or long skewer, poke 100 holes into the entire surface of the cake. Slowly pour syrup over warm cake.
7. Serve garnished with crème fraîche or sour cream. Top with candied orange peel.

Chef Chat—

*Marsala is a fortified wine from Italy that is drunk as a dessert wine but also used in the preparation of zabaglione and tiramisu. A domestic version is available, but I recommend looking for the imported brands—it's worth the five or six extra dollars.

Can you use the lavender growing in the backyard for this recipe? Absolutely, if you are certain that it is a culinary variety and has not been sprayed with any pesticides. Pick the flowers and wash them under cold water and allow them to dry. Look for local lavender at your farmers market as well.

savoring
wild salmon

– Menu –

• Quick-Cured Smoked Salmon with Hot Mustard
Sauce and Fresh Herb Blue Corn Blini •
• Pecan- and Herb-Crusted Salmon •
• Salmon and Fennel en Papillote •
• Steamed Salmon Dumplings •

Rich in vitamin A, the B-group vitamins, and Omega 3 fatty acids that doctors tell us we should consume regularly, salmon is a terrific full-flavored fish that stands up to grilling, poaching, and saucing. A friend turned me on to a source for wild salmon—www.vitalchoice.com—that has an amazing selection of Alaskan salmon and other seafood products—including halibut, sablefish, albacore tuna, scallops, and more—shrink-wrap-sealed and carefully shipped on dry ice. The downside to wild salmon is if it is caught when very large, there can be copious amounts of mercury in the flesh, a health no-no especially if you are pregnant. Vital Choice guarantees their products are as free from contaminates as possible, and wild is preferable to farm-raised salmon, which are loaded with antibiotics, pesticides, synthetic coloring agents, growth hormones, and GMOs. My favorite saying about salmon is "it's good and good for you." There are many varieties of salmon—Sockeye, Chinook, King, Coho, and Silver, to name a few—but I have never noticed a big difference in the recipe outcome with varying the type I use. Play with the different varieties you find in your local fish markets and see what rocks your (salmon fishing) boat. •

facing: Cured and smoked wild salmon

Quick-Cured Smoked Salmon with Hot Mustard Sauce and Fresh Herb Blue Corn Blini

The Swedes knew that curing salmon in a mixture of sugar and coarse salt not only preserved the prized fish but that, by adding sprigs of dill to the curing process, the fish was also delicious when thinly sliced, as it is traditionally served. I gave the traditional cure mixture a Santa Fe spin by adding caribe chile flakes, which give it a kick, and by using brown sugar instead of white, which gives it an almost barbecue flavor when the fish is smoked. If you don't smoke the salmon, leave the cure on for 3 days, and then slice it and serve as gravlax.

Makes 2 pounds cured salmon

2 pounds fresh salmon, whole sides

1/4 cup kosher salt

3/4 cup dark brown sugar

4 teaspoons caribe chile

Freshly ground pepper

1. Check salmon for pin bones and remove with needle-nose pliers or tweezers.
2. In a large, nonreactive oblong pan, mix salt and sugar until well blended and spread it out into a shape that will facilitate the most contact to the salmon flesh. Sprinkle caribe chile over salt-sugar mixture.
3. Season salmon with freshly ground pepper and lay it flesh side down onto prepared cure mixture.
4. Cover with plastic wrap and place a similar-sized pan directly onto salmon. Weigh down pan with canned goods or brick and refrigerate for 24 hours.
5. Remove salmon from the marinade and gently scrape off a majority of the marinade.
6. Prepare the smoker and smoke salmon for 8 to 12 minutes, depending on the thickness of the flesh,* using a mild wood (alder, apple, pecan, or cherry).
7. Serve at room temperature with Hot Mustard Sauce.

Smoking times: 8 minutes for salmon up to 1 inch thick • 10 minutes for up to 2 inches thick • 12 minutes for thicker than 2 inches

Hot Mustard Sauce

1/2 cup sour cream

1/4 cup hot mustard, any style (Chinese preferred)

1 garlic clove, minced

1/2 teaspoon kosher salt

1/2 teaspoon freshly ground pepper

1 scallion, minced, tops and root ends discarded

1 teaspoon fresh lime juice

Chef Chat—
Make delicious canapés by spreading a thin layer of the mustard sauce onto the Herb Blue Corn Blini (page 58) and top with a piece of smoked salmon that you have flaked with a fork. Garnish with chopped chives.

1. Mix all ingredients together in a medium bowl and chill for 1 hour.

above: John teaches John a smoking technique

Fresh Herb Blue Corn Blini

Makes approximately 40 blini

1/2 cup blue corn flour

1/2 cup flour

1 teaspoon baking powder

1/2 teaspoon baking soda

1-1/2 cups buttermilk

2 tablespoons melted butter, plus additional
   for buttering skillet

1 egg

1 teaspoon finely chopped fresh dill

1 teaspoon finely chopped chives

1 teaspoon finely chopped thyme

1. Mix all ingredients together in a medium bowl and blend until smooth. Mixture should be the consistency of pancake batter; add additional buttermilk if it is too thick.

2. Heat a large skillet over medium heat and lightly butter it. Form 2-inch pancakes by pouring 1 tablespoon batter onto the pan. Allow blini to cook until batter starts to bubble. Flip blini and cook second side until lightly browned. Continue process until you have used all of the batter.

3. Place blini on a plate and allow to cool before spreading with toppings.

Pecan- and Herb-Crusted Salmon

You'll notice this crumb mixture is similar to the one used on the Pecan-Crusted Rack of Lamb (see page 30). It works equally well on both dishes.

Serves 6

6 salmon fillets, 5 to 6 ounces each, skinned

1 tablespoon olive oil

Salt and pepper, to season

1/4 cup Dijon mustard

1/2 cup finely chopped toasted pecans

1/4 cup plain breadcrumbs

1 teaspoon kosher salt

1 teaspoon freshly ground pepper

2 tablespoons lemon zest

1/4 cup capers, rinsed if salted

1 tablespoon chopped fresh parsley

1 tablespoon chopped fresh dill

1 tablespoon chopped fresh thyme

1. Brush fillets with olive oil and season with salt and pepper. Place salmon in a roasting pan, flesh side up, and smear with mustard.

2. In a medium bowl combine remaining ingredients. Mix well and then pat mixture onto mustard-spread fish, pressing well to keep it in place.

3. Preheat oven to 450 degrees F. Place salmon into oven, crumbed side up, and immediately lower temperature to 400 degrees F. Bake for 10 to 12 minutes or until the fish loses it translucency. Serve immediately with Green Chile and Cheddar Polenta (page 109) or buttery mashed potatoes.

above: Johnny Vee loves salmon

Salmon and Fennel en Papillote

Beautiful and dramatic in its presentation, fish prepared in this classic French way of cooking will impress your guests. Make the packages ahead of time and chill; then add 5 minutes to the baking time listed here.

Serves 6

6 salmon fillets, 6 ounces each, skinned
1 teaspoon kosher salt
1 teaspoon freshly ground pepper
1 bulb fennel, sliced thin
1 small sweet onion, sliced thin
1 large carrot, cut into fine julienne
1 cup thinly sliced shiitake mushrooms
24 flat-leaf parsley leaves
6 teaspoons unsalted butter
6 teaspoons finely julienned orange peel
6 teaspoons dry vermouth or dry white wine
Vegetable oil

1. Preheat oven to 425 degrees F. Season both sides of the fish fillets with salt and pepper. Cut 6 pieces of parchment paper 12 x 18 inches. Fold paper in half and cut each piece in the shape of an oval flying saucer that is 16 inches across and 12 inches from top to bottom (see photos pages 62–63).

2. Place fish in center of one side of the parchment paper. Scatter vegetables and parsley over fillets and dot the top of each with 1 teaspoon butter and 1 teaspoon orange peel. Splash 1 teaspoon of vermouth or wine over each fillet.

3. Fold paper over fish and pleat to seal papillote along entire diameter of the paper, finishing with a small twist at the end of fold.

4. Brush surface of paper with vegetable oil and place on baking sheet.

5. Bake 8 to 12 minutes depending on thickness of fish fillet. Carefully peel back paper and serve immediately.

Chef Chat—
To make this dish extra special, make an orange
butter sauce by preparing the Beurre Blanc recipe
on page 161 and substituting fresh-squeezed
orange juice for the white wine. Serve the sauce on
the side so guests can ladle it over the fish after
opening the papillote.

above: Papillote prep

above: Ready to fold and seal

Steamed Salmon Dumplings

Mu Du Noodles is my favorite Santa Fe Pan-Asian restaurant. Chef and owner Mu Jing Lau has taught many classes for me, and this quick dumpling is one of her special recipes. Thanks, Mu!

Serves 6 to 8

1 pound salmon, coarsely chopped

1 egg

1-1/2 teaspoons sugar

1/2 teaspoon white pepper

2 tablespoons Thai fish sauce

2 scallions, minced, tops and root ends discarded

1/2 cup peeled and deveined shrimp, any size

1 package wonton wrappers

4 large cabbage leaves

1. Place salmon, egg, sugar, pepper, fish sauce, scallion, and shrimp in a food processor fitted with a steel blade attachment. Pulse the mixture a few times to combine the ingredients but do not overprocess. You should have a spreadable mixture with a few very small visible chunks.
2. Using a round biscuit or cookie cutter, cut the wonton wrappers into 3-inch rounds. Take a teaspoon of filling and spread onto each wrapper. Draw wrapper toward the center of itself to create a dumpling and tap gently on counter to create a flat bottom.
3. Place cabbage leaves in a bamboo steamer and place dumplings on cabbage.
4. Cover and steam over boiling water until dumplings are opaque, about 10 minutes. Serve immediately with soy sauce that has been drizzled with a little sesame oil.

facing: Delicious dumplings
above: Time to eat

shrimply delicious

CRAVING CRUSTACEANS

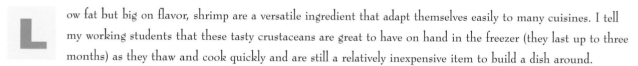

– Menu –

• Garlic Shrimp with Chiles de Arbol • Smoked Shrimp Salad • Real Shrimp Toast •
• Overnight Buttermilk Waffles with Creamy Smoked Shrimp Sauce •
• Smoked Artichoke and Shrimp Dip • Thai-Marinated Grilled Shrimp •
• Shrimp and Coconut Fritters •

Low fat but big on flavor, shrimp are a versatile ingredient that adapt themselves easily to many cuisines. I tell my working students that these tasty crustaceans are great to have on hand in the freezer (they last up to three months) as they thaw and cook quickly and are still a relatively inexpensive item to build a dish around. There are hundreds of species of shrimp, but most can be divided into two categories: warm-water shrimp and cold-water shrimp. Their colors vary widely as well, ranging from grayish-white to bright red.

The flavor is similar throughout America's most popular shellfish. Shrimp are sold by size in groupings that refer to how many shrimp would be in a pound. General size categories include colossal (10 or less), jumbo (11–15), extra-large (16–20), large (21–30), medium (31–35), small (36–45), and miniature (about 100).

Choose your shrimp size by recipe use: jumbos and extra-large are perfect for shrimp cocktail. But if the shrimp are going to be chopped for a shu mai filling, buy the most cost-effective ones.

A little trick restaurateurs play on customers is to cut the shrimp in half along the back—when the two halves cook they curl up and it looks like two shrimp. Bigger shrimp are not necessarily better; even shrimpy, scrimpy shrimp are scrumptious. •

facing: Thai-Marinated Grilled Shrimp

Garlic Shrimp with Chiles de Arbol

Serves 4 as an appetizer

3/4 cup Spanish olive oil

8 garlic cloves, sliced thin*

1 pound small shrimp (size 36–45), peeled

1 teaspoon crushed chiles de arbol, or to taste

Pinch of kosher salt

2 tablespoons chopped parsley

1 lime, cut into wedges

1 pound loaf crusty bread, toasted in oven

1. Heat olive oil in medium saucepan over medium heat until very hot but not smoking.
2. Add garlic slices and allow to sizzle for 1 minute.
3. Add shrimp, chiles de arbol, salt, and parsley. Stir once and pour into a heated ovenproof dish. Serve immediately, garnished with lime wedges, and with crusty bread on the side.

To serve as a main course, toss finished shrimp with cooked linguini. Garnish with additional chopped parsley and grated Parmesan cheese.

*Gadget Gab—for perfect razor-thin slices use the Messermeister garlic slicer.

Smoked Shrimp Salad

More great smoky flavor, this time in a delicious salad.

Serves 6

2 cups medium shrimp, about 1/2 pound

3/4 cup finely diced celery

1/2 cup finely diced red bell pepper

1/2 cup finely diced yellow bell pepper

1/4 cup finely diced green bell pepper

1/2 cup chopped scallions, tops and root ends discarded

2 teaspoons freshly squeezed lime juice

1 teaspoon salt

1 teaspoon freshly ground pepper

1 teaspoon smoked Spanish paprika

1/2 cup mayonnaise, or to taste

1. Smoke the shrimp for 6 minutes using the mildest wood available (such as alder, cherry, or apple).

2. Allow to cool, and then peel and slice along the back of each shrimp.

3. In a medium bowl, mix celery, bell peppers, scallions, lime juice, salt, pepper, and paprika.

4. Add shrimp and mayonnaise and toss well. Allow salad to sit refrigerated for at least 1/2 hour for flavors to meld. Garnish with an additional pinch of paprika and serve as a stuffing for whole tomatoes with the seeds scooped out, or as a filling for a sandwich.

Real Shrimp Toast

This classic Chinese appetizer is a favorite from my youth. Easy to make and oh, so yummy.

Serves 6 (3 pieces each)

9 slices soft white bread (like Wonder bread)
9 medium shrimp, peeled, deveined, and sliced in half along the back
2 tablespoons cornstarch
18 cilantro leaves
Oil for frying

For the Shrimp Paste:

1/2 pound medium shrimp, peeled and deveined
1/2 teaspoon salt
2 teaspoons rice vinegar
1/2 teaspoon toasted sesame oil
1 tablespoon cornstarch
1/2 teaspoon white pepper
1 egg white

1. Trim crusts off bread and slice in half diagonally.
2. Prepare the shrimp paste by placing ingredients in food processor fitted with a steel blade. Pulse the mixture a few times until shrimp are finely minced but still have some texture.
3. Spread shrimp mixture evenly on bread triangles.
4. Dip each piece of the remaining sliced shrimp in cornstarch and press into shrimp paste mixture in the center of the bread slice. Stick a leaf of cilantro next to the shrimp.
5. Heat oil in wok to 350 degrees F. Deep-fry toast pieces, shrimp side down, for 45 seconds; then carefully turn them over using a slotted spoon and fry 15 seconds longer. Drain on paper towels and serve immediately.

Overnight Buttermilk Waffles with Creamy Smoked Shrimp Sauce

These savory waffles are perfect for brunch or supper. Not a waffle fan? Serve the creamy smoked shrimp sauce over toast.

Serves 4 to 6

2 cups flour

1 teaspoon sugar

1/2 teaspoon salt

1/2 teaspoon dry yeast

2 1/4 cups buttermilk

1/2 cup butter, melted and cooled to
    room temperature

2 eggs

Vegetable oil

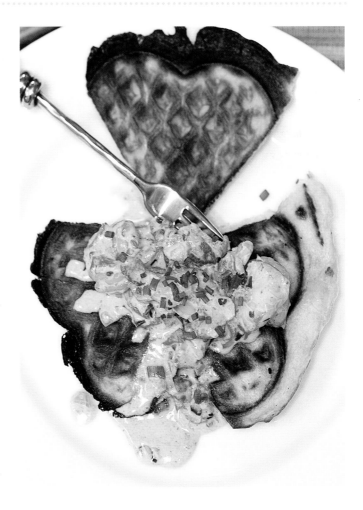

1. The night before making the waffles, combine the dry ingredients and yeast in a medium bowl. Stir in the buttermilk and melted butter; mix well. Cover with plastic wrap and leave at room temperature overnight or up to 12 hours.

2. To cook waffles, heat waffle iron and brush with vegetable oil. Separate eggs and stir the yolks into the batter. Whip the whites to soft peaks and gently fold into the batter.

3. Pour a ladleful of batter onto the waffle iron and close lid, cooking for 3 to 5 minutes, depending on waffle iron instructions. Serve waffles hot with Creamy Smoked Shrimp Sauce.

Creamy Smoked Shrimp Sauce

2 cups medium shrimp, unpeeled, about 1/2 pound

8 ounces thick-cut bacon

2 tablespoons butter

2 shallots, finely chopped

4 scallions, chopped, tops and root ends discarded

1 teaspoon fresh thyme

2 Roma tomatoes, diced, seeds discarded

Juice of 1/2 lemon

1/4 cup fish stock or clam juice

1-1/2 cups heavy cream

Pinch smoked Spanish paprika

Salt and pepper, to taste

1. Smoke the shrimp for 6 minutes using the mildest wood available such as alder, cherry, or apple.* Allow to cool, and then peel and slice along the back of each shrimp.

2. Cut the bacon into 1/4-inch slices and sauté in a medium saucepan until crispy. Drain on paper towels and drain the fat from the pan. Add the butter to the pan and sauté the shallots and scallions for 4 minutes over medium heat.

3. Add the thyme, tomatoes, lemon juice, and fish stock, and sauté briefly. Add cream and reduce to a simmer. Add the shrimp and cook until the sauce thickens slightly.

4. Stir in the bacon and paprika; season with salt and pepper. Serve hot over Overnight Buttermilk Waffles, toast, biscuits, or grits.

*Gadget Gab—Try the Camerons Stovetop Smoker. The smoker can be used indoors on gas, electric, and glass-top stoves with minimal ventilation necessary.

Smoked Artichoke and Shrimp Dip

Another throwback to my youth in Rochester, New York—given a smoky spin by smoking the artichoke hearts and the shrimp.

Makes 3 cups

1 cup diced smoked artichoke hearts*

1 cup finely chopped smoked shrimp*

1/2 cup mayonnaise

1/2 cup sour cream

1/4 cup grated Parmesan cheese

Pinch smoked Spanish paprika

1 teaspoon hot sauce, or to taste

1 teaspoon chopped chives for garnish

1. Combine all ingredients except the chives in a medium bowl and mix well.
2. Place dip in an ovenproof serving dish. Bake at 375 degrees F in the upper part of a preheated oven for 20 to 25 minutes, until dip is nicely browned and bubbling.
3. Garnish with chopped chives and serve with assorted crackers or crispy baguettes.

Smoke the shrimp and artichokes together for 6 minutes in the Camerons Stovetop Smoker using a mild wood such as alder, apple, cherry, or pecan.

above: Smoked shrimp and artichokes

Thai-Marinated Grilled Shrimp

The great flavors of Thai cooking glaze the shrimp when they are grilled.

Serves 8

2 pounds thawed shrimp, peeled and deveined

For the Marinade:

1/4 cup chopped fresh mint

1/4 cup chopped fresh cilantro

2 teaspoons hot red chili sauce such as Sambal Olek,*
or to taste

4 teaspoons soy sauce

4 teaspoons freshly squeezed lime juice

2 stalks lemongrass, rough chopped

2 inches fresh ginger, peeled and grated

2 teaspoons sugar

2 tablespoons water

1. Combine all ingredients for the marinade in a medium bowl. Stir to combine well.
2. Toss shrimp in marinade. Let stand at room temperature for up to 1 hour.
3. Prepare the grill and grill shrimp over direct heat until shrimp are just pink. Serve immediately.

Available in most Asian markets.

Chef Chat—
This marinade can also be tossed with thawed, pre-cooked shrimp that have been thawed and served after marinating for 30 minutes. Serve as a cold appetizer.

above: Smoky shrimp

Shrimp and Coconut Fritters

This recipe was inspired by a version I found in a Cuban cookbook that called for conch meat. Shrimp are more accessible and tastier.

Serves 8

1 pound medium shrimp, peeled and deveined

1/2 cup grated fresh coconut

3 scallions, thinly sliced, tops and root ends discarded

2 garlic cloves, minced

1/2 red bell pepper, minced

2 teaspoons minced cilantro leaves

2 teaspoons fresh lime juice

1 teaspoon lime zest*

2 tablespoons peanut oil, plus 6 cups for frying

1-1/2 cups flour

1/4 cup yellow cornmeal

1 teaspoon baking powder

1 teaspoon salt

1 teaspoon freshly ground pepper

1/2 teaspoon cayenne

4 eggs, separated

1/2 to 3/4 cup milk

4 limes, quartered

1. Quick-pulse shrimp in food processor fitted with a steel blade until finely chopped but with a little texture remaining.
2. Mix shrimp in a large bowl with coconut, scallions, garlic, bell pepper, cilantro, lime juice, lime zest, and 2 tablespoons of peanut oil.
3. Mix dry ingredients together in a medium bowl. Beat egg yolks into 1/2 cup of milk and add to dry ingredients. Add shrimp mixture and mix to form a soft dough. If it's too thick, add more milk.
4. Beat egg whites in medium bowl until stiff peaks form. Fold one-third of whites into batter, and then gently fold in remaining whites.
5. Place 6 cups peanut oil in a large wok or deep saucepan and heat to 375 degrees F. Make heaping tablespoons of batter and carefully drop into heated oil, frying fritters in batches so as not to crowd the pan. Turn fritters several times and fry until golden brown. Transfer to paper towels and serve hot, garnished with fresh lime wedges for squeezing.

*Gadget Gab—the microplane zester makes this job a breeze.

flamin' tonsils
and smokin' ears

FOOD THAT BITES BACK

— Menu —

• Little Fried "Mice" •

• Nuoc Cham (Vietnamese Vinaigrette) •

• Chile Rellenos •

• Spicy Indonesian Chicken Laksa •

• Malaysian Green Chile Vegetable Curry •

• Tomato and Jalapeño Sorbet •

• Hot-Hot Mexican Chocolate Sauce •

What's better than spicy food? It stimulates the endorphins in the brain and makes your taste buds stand up and take notice. I think it's interesting that people in most countries having a hot tropical climate love spicy food. There's a school of thought that says as the sweat appears on your brow while you're consuming fiery foods, a built-in air-conditioning unit kicks in and cools the body. Whatever the reason, professed chile-heads will love these dishes that bite back! •

facing: Matthew's Little Fried "Mice"

Little Fried "Mice"

After eating these fiery little jalapeño poppers, you will need a beer (or two) to put out the fire. No, they're not really mice . . . but they look like 'em.

Serves 6

18 whole pickled jalapeños, stem on, juice reserved

1/4 cup salted peanuts

1/2 cup chopped cooked chicken thigh meat

3 scallions, chopped, tops and root ends discarded

1/4 cup grated Cheddar cheese

2 tablespoons reserved jalapeño pickle juice

3 cups vegetable oil

1/4 cup flour

1 recipe Beer Batter (page 83)

1. Drain jalapeños, reserving the juice. Slit jalapeños from stem to bottom using a small paring knife.
2. Finely chop peanuts and then place in a food processor work bowl fitted with a steel blade. Add chicken, scallions, cheese, and pickle juice, and quick pulse to make a moist stuffing.
3. Stuff jalapeños with 1 teaspoon of the stuffing and squeeze closed as tightly as possible.
4. Heat oil to 350 degrees F in a deep skillet or wok. Dust stuffed "mice" with flour and dip in Beer Batter (see page 83) using chopsticks or tongs.
5. Fry "mice" in batches and drain on paper towels. Serve hot with Sinus-Shattering Horseradish Dipping Sauce.

Sinus-Shattering Horseradish Dipping Sauce

Serves 6

1-1/4 cups orange marmalade

1 tablespoon minced shallot

2 tablespoons hot English mustard

2 tablespoons prepared horseradish

1. Whisk all ingredients together in a medium bowl, cover, and chill.

Nuoc Cham (Vietnamese Vinaigrette)

Sweet, sour, salty, and spicy—all the flavors we love in Asian cookery, and all in this vinaigrette.

Makes 3/4 cup

3 red Thai chiles, stemmed and chopped

1 large clove garlic

1 teaspoon grated peeled ginger

1 tablespoon coconut palm sugar or brown sugar

4 teaspoons fresh lime juice

4 teaspoons rice vinegar

3 tablespoons water

3 tablespoons Thai fish sauce

1. Using a mortar and pestle, mash together chiles, garlic, and ginger into a fine paste. Add the palm sugar and combine.
2. Place paste into a medium mixing bowl and add remaining ingredients. Whisk until well blended.

Chef Chat—

This luscious sauce is based on nuoc mam. It is great on a cucumber salad as well as for a dip for Vietnamese spring rolls. One guest chef offered a story that it is served in Thailand with sticky rice rolled into small balls and eaten as a snack. Folklore says that if your rice ball falls apart in the sauce, you may have bad luck.

Chile Rellenos

These stuffed chiles are one of my favorite New Mexican dishes. Try all three batters and choose your favorite.

Serves 6

8 ounces cold sharp Cheddar cheese

6 large whole New Mexican green chiles, roasted and peeled

1 batch batter (Blue Corn Buttermilk Batter, below; Soufflé Relleno Batter, page 83; or Beer Batter, page 83)

3 cups vegetable oil for frying

1. Cut cheese into matchstick-size pieces, 2 inches long by 1/8-inch square. Cut a tiny slit toward the top of the chile and carefully slide in pieces of the cheese until chile is filled with cheese.

2. Drain stuffed chiles on paper towel before dipping in batter. Heat oil to 350 degrees F. Dip chiles into batter and carefully slide them into the heated oil. Once they are golden brown, turn chiles over. The second side will brown more quickly. Reserve leftover batter for another use.

3. Drain on paper towels and serve warm with Red Chile Sauce (see page 167).

Blue Corn Buttermilk Batter

1 cup blue cornmeal

3/4 cup flour

1 teaspoon baking powder

1/2 teaspoon sugar

1/2 teaspoon salt

About 1-1/4 cups buttermilk

2 eggs

Chef Chat—
Rellenos can be held in a low oven (150 degrees) for 30 minutes but are best served immediately as the batter will lose its crunch.

1. Combine dry ingredients in a medium bowl.
2. Whisk together buttermilk and eggs in a small bowl and then add to dry ingredients.
3. Mix to make a smooth batter, adding more buttermilk if necessary. Batter should be the density of pancake batter.
4. Allow to rest 10 minutes before using.

Soufflé Relleno Batter

1/4 cup plus 2 teaspoons flour

3/4 teaspoon baking powder

1/4 teaspoon salt

4 eggs, separated

1/4 teaspoon cream of tartar

1. Combine flour, baking powder, and salt in a small bowl.
2. Beat egg whites in a medium bowl with cream of tartar, until stiff but not dry.
3. Add the egg yolks, one at a time, to the whites, beating after each addition. Gently fold in dry ingredients.
4. Use batter immediately.

Beer Batter

3/4 cup plus 2 teaspoons flour

1/4 cup cornstarch

1/2 teaspoon salt

1/4 teaspoon cumin

1/4 teaspoon cayenne

1 cup beer, any brand except dark beer

1. Combine flour, cornstarch, salt, cumin, and cayenne in medium bowl.
2. Measure beer into tilted measuring cup to be sure you have 1 cup liquid. Stir in beer and foam and whisk batter until smooth.
3. Allow batter to rest for 20 minutes before using.
4. If a thinner batter is desired, add a small amount of additional beer.

Chef Chat—
Students are always asking me if it's possible to bake a batter-coated relleno. The Blue Corn Buttermilk Batter does bake well by spraying a baking sheet generously with cooking spray and then laying the dipped relleno onto it. Spray the relleno lightly with the cooking spray and bake at 400 degrees F until it is nicely browned, about 12 minutes. This is the only batter that works in this manner. The rest should be deep-fried.

Spicy Indonesian Chicken Laksa

Curry laksa is a spicy noodle soup that may take its name from the Sanskrit word laksha *meaning "many"—referring to the many delicious ingredients in the soup. Laksa can have shrimp, fish, or chicken as its main ingredient.*

Serves 6

6 cups chicken stock

1 (3-inch) piece fresh ginger, sliced into 8 pieces

Juice of 2 lemons

12 kaffir lime leaves

2 cans (14.5 ounces each) coconut milk

2 tablespoons tamarind paste

2 lemongrass stalks, trimmed and cut into 2-inch slices

3 tablespoons coconut palm sugar or brown sugar

2 tablespoons Thai fish sauce

8 ounces shiitake mushrooms, sliced

1/4 cup Thai basil leaves, torn into small pieces

1 small head Napa cabbage, sliced

1 pound boneless, skinless chicken breasts, cut into 1-inch squares

1 (7-ounce) package rice vermicelli noodles, cooked according to package instructions

2 tablespoons cilantro leaves

6 small Thai chiles, seeded and chopped

1. Combine stock, ginger, and lemon juice in a large soup pot.
2. Remove stems from lime leaves and add leaves to pot. Gradually bring stock to a boil over medium heat.
3. Stir in coconut milk and return to boil. Add tamarind paste, lemongrass, palm sugar, and fish sauce; stir until sugar dissolves.
4. Add mushrooms, basil, and cabbage, and simmer until tender, about 8 minutes. Add chicken. Cook until chicken is cooked through, about 5 minutes. Stir in cooked rice noodles.
5. Float cilantro and chiles in soup for serving.

Chef Chat—
Remember to tell your guests to eat around the lime leaves, lemongrass, and ginger pieces—they will be too woody and leafy to digest. Kaffir lime leaves and lemongrass may be stored in the freezer in ziplock bags and thawed briefly before adding to dishes. Coconut palm sugar has a tendency to harden in the cupboard; zapping it briefly in the microwave before using will soften it. If your tamarind paste is in a block, break off a hunk and pour 1/4 cup hot water over it. Work it with your fingers to soften it and remove any seeds you come across. Add to the laksa with the water in which it was dissolved. You may also substitute tamarind sauce for the paste—use the same amount.

Malaysian Green Chile Vegetable Curry

Serves 12

3 tablespoons peanut oil

2 onions, chopped

3 garlic cloves, minced

3 zucchini, cut into 1-inch chunks

3 Thai eggplant, cut into 1-inch chunks

1 leek, roughly chopped and rinsed well

2 poblano chiles, roasted, peeled, seeded, and cut
 into 1-inch squares

1 small head broccoli, cut into florets

1 cup chopped green cabbage

3 tablespoons hot curry powder

1 cup vegetable stock

1/2 cup coconut palm sugar or dark brown sugar

2/3 cup chunky peanut butter

2 tablespoons nam pla Thai fish sauce

Fresh cilantro sprigs

1. Heat peanut oil in a large heavy skillet and sauté onions until they start to brown. Add garlic and cook for 2 minutes.

2. Add remaining vegetables and cook over medium heat, stirring occasionally, until they become tender, about
   12 minutes.

3. Sprinkle curry powder over vegetables and stir until it is completely incorporated. Add stock, palm sugar, and peanut
   butter; mix well.

4. Reduce heat to low, cover, and allow curry to simmer for 15 minutes. Stir in fish sauce and garnish with sprigs of
   cilantro just before serving.

Chef Chat—

Fragrant in a stinky way, fish sauce is an important ingredient in Asian cooking; resist the temptation to leave it out. When shopping for it, look for a brand that is in a glass rather than in a plastic bottle. I like the Squid brand. Fish sauce from Vietnam is called nuoc nam; *if it comes from the Philippines it is called* patis. *They may be used interchangeably. Years ago I did a class using recipes that were unearthed from Pompeii. An ingredient called garum was used in many of the recipes in place of salt. It was popular in the Roman Empire. I learned that garum was a fish-sauce-like condiment that was made from dried fish with the addition of pepper, oil, wine, and herbs, including lovage and dill. If you are cooking for vegetarians or vegans you may substitute the same amount of soy sauce for the fish sauce.*

Tomato and Jalapeño Sorbet

This is a refreshing summer dessert that can also be served as a palate-cleansing course when you want to wake up your dinner guests and prepare them for the next dish. I have served a small scoop as an intriguing garnish atop a bowl of gazpacho or as a clever cocktail, set afloat in frozen vodka in an elegant martini glass!

Serves 6 to 8

3/4 cup sugar

5 cups tomato juice

1/2 teaspoon finely grated fresh lime zest

2 seeded and minced jalapeños, or more

1 teaspoon sherry vinegar, or to taste

1. Bring sugar, tomato juice, zest, and jalapeños to a boil in a medium heavy saucepan, stirring until sugar is dissolved.

2. Reduce heat and simmer 5 minutes. Pour mixture into a blender, then add sherry vinegar and blend until smooth. Be careful pureeing hot liquids—placing a tea towel over the lid of the blender will prevent the lid from flying off! Pour the puree through a fine-mesh sieve into a large bowl, pressing pulp and discarding any remaining solids. Chill mixture completely.

3. Pour mixture into ice cream freezer and freeze according to manufacturer's instructions. Transfer to an airtight container and freeze until firm.

Hot-Hot Mexican Chocolate Sauce

Chocolate and chiles have been combined and savored together going all the way back to the Mayan civilization. They are a natural marriage of flavor in the delicious moles of Mexico and in this sweet-hot sauce. Try it over the creamy Dulce de Leche Ice Cream on page 124.

Serves 6

6 ounces bittersweet chocolate, chopped

2/3 cup heavy cream

3/4 teaspoon ground cinnamon

1 tablespoon hot ground red chile

Pinch salt

1. Place chocolate, cream, and cinnamon in a medium metal bowl set over a saucepan of simmering water. Stir until chocolate has melted and mixture is smooth.

2. Stir in chile and salt. Cover sauce and refrigerate. To serve, warm sauce over a small pan of water over low heat, or in the microwave.

Chef Chat—
For true chocolate-chile decadence, use this sauce to plate the Chocolate Pine Nut Tacos on page 154.

above: A chile-loving family

the art of the artichoke

DELICIOUS THISTLE

– Menu –

• Cream of Artichoke Soup •

• Lemon, Artichoke, and Fennel Salad with Shaved Parmesan •

• Beer-Battered Artichoke Fritters with Horseradish Sauce •

• Artichoke Ravioli with Lemon and Parmesan-Cream Sauce •

I wonder who first discovered that this fascinating member of the thistle family was edible and was brave enough to eat it. In A.D. 77, Roman scholar Gaius Plinius Secundus wrote a thirty-seven-volume encyclopedia of natural history called *Historia Naturalis* and in it proclaims, "The artichoke is one of the earth's monstrosities," despite its popularity among Roman gastronomes.

A cookbook called *Directions for Cookery* by Eliza Leslie published in 1828 taught Americans how to prepare the then-exotic vegetable. By 1900, five hundred acres of California farmland were planted with chokes, and eventually the town of Castroville produced 75 percent of the U.S. crop.

The artichoke's sharp, tart taste makes it excellent for saucing and frying, and the once-ubiquitous steamed artichoke with melted butter as an appetizer is slowly reappearing on restaurant menus. Trim the tips of the leaves, steam the artichokes, and devour the bite of flesh at the bottom of each leaf.

Savor the heart once the thorny choke has been removed. Baby artichokes can be completely consumed, simply grilled and drizzled with olive oil and a splash of lemon juice. Fresh are best; look for medium size as the enormous ones can become tough. I prefer frozen over canned hearts, but canned hearts are fine in salads. •

facing: Versatile, edible thistle

Cream of Artichoke Soup

8 large artichoke hearts from steamed and trimmed artichokes, or 8 canned whole artichoke hearts

2 tablespoons butter

1 large baking potato, peeled and diced

4 garlic cloves, chopped

Juice of 2 lemons

6 cups chicken or vegetable stock

1/2 cup heavy cream

Salt and freshly ground pepper, to taste

2 teaspoons fresh thyme leaves

1. Scrape the small amount of artichoke pulp from the bottom of each artichoke leaf and reserve. Dice artichoke hearts.

2. Melt butter in a large soup pot and allow to brown slightly. Add diced artichoke hearts, reserved pulp, potato, and garlic, and sauté for 5 minutes or until potato and artichokes are partially cooked.

3. Add lemon juice and stock, and bring to a boil. Reduce heat and simmer for 15 to 20 minutes or until vegetables are tender.

4. Purée the soup in batches in a blender and return to soup pot. Stir in the cream. Season with salt and pepper and ladle soup into warmed bowls. Garnish with fresh thyme.

Lemon, Artichoke, and Fennel Salad
with Shaved Parmesan

Serves 4

2 cups thinly sliced artichoke hearts (fresh or canned)

1 large fennel bulb, trimmed and thinly sliced*

Juice of 1 lemon

2 teaspoons extra virgin olive oil

2 ounces Parmigiano-Reggiano, thinly shaved

Sea salt and freshly ground pepper, to taste

1. Toss all ingredients except the Parmigiano and salt and pepper in a medium bowl.
2. Gently add Parmigiano and scatter salad on serving platter.
3. Season with salt and pepper and serve immediately.

*Gadget Gab—There are a variety of mandolins available that make this job a breeze. The thinner the slices of fennel, the more delicate the salad will be. I prefer the Rosle mandoline and recommend using a Mani-Kare cut-resistant glove to protect those fingers.

Beer-Battered Artichoke Fritters
with Horseradish Sauce

In Italy, tiny fresh baby artichokes are used for this recipe. Frozen hearts are much more accessible and work just fine.

Serves 4 as an appetizer

3/4 cup plus 1/4 cup flour

1/4 cup cornstarch

1/2 teaspoon kosher salt

1/4 teaspoon toasted and ground cumin seed

1/4 teaspoon cayenne

1 cup beer, any brand, preferably not a dark beer

24 frozen artichoke hearts

3 cups vegetable oil

2 lemons cut into wedges

1. Combine 3/4 cup flour and cornstarch in a medium bowl.
2. Stir in salt, cumin, and cayenne.
3. Measure beer into tilted measuring cup to ensure that you have 1 cup liquid. Stir beer and foam into flour mixture and whisk batter until smooth.
4. Allow batter to rest for 20 minutes before using. If a thinner batter is desired, add a small amount of beer.
5. Lightly season artichoke hearts with salt and pepper.
6. Heat the oil to 350 degrees F in a wok or deep skillet. Dust artichokes with remaining 1/4 cup flour, dip into batter, and allow to drain briefly. Working in batches, fry fritters until golden brown. Using a slotted spoon, drain fritters and scatter on paper towels; lightly salt. Serve warm with lemon wedges and Horseradish Sauce.

Horseradish Sauce

1/2 cup sour cream

2 tablespoons freshly grated horseradish root, or

    2 teaspoons prepared horseradish

1 teaspoon freshly squeezed lime juice

Pinch salt

Freshly ground pepper

1. Combine all ingredients in medium mixing bowl. Cover and chill.

Artichoke Ravioli with
Lemon and Parmesan-Cream Sauce

The tartness of the artichokes and the lemon make a perfect marriage of flavor in these homemade ravioli.

Serves 6

For the Filling:

1 tablespoon olive oil

1 cup diced artichoke hearts, fresh, canned, or frozen

2 garlic cloves, minced

1 cup drained whole-milk Ricotta cheese

1/4 cup grated Parmigiano-Reggiano cheese

1/4 cup minced parsley

1 teaspoon salt

1 teaspoon freshly ground pepper

1. Heat olive oil in medium saucepan and sauté artichoke hearts and garlic until slightly browned.
2. Place artichokes in medium bowl and add ricotta, Parmigiano, parsley, salt, and pepper. Mix to combine.

For the Pasta Dough:

2 cups all-purpose flour

3 extra large eggs

1. Place flour in a food processor fitted with a metal blade.
2. Mix eggs together in a small bowl and add to flour all at once.
3. Pulse-mix the dough until it forms a ball.
4. Remove dough from bowl (being careful of processor blade), knead briefly, wrap in plastic wrap, and allow to rest for 15 minutes.

above: Simply served with butter
below: Get cookin'

Lemon and Parmesan-Cream Sauce

2 cups heavy cream
4 garlic cloves, minced
1/4 cup vermouth
2 teaspoons lemon zest
1/2 cup grated Parmigiano-Reggiano cheese
Pinch ground nutmeg
Kosher salt and freshly ground pepper, to taste

1. Place cream and garlic in medium saucepan and bring to a boil. Reduce to simmer and allow to cook until cream has reduced to 1 cup.
2. Whisk in vermouth, lemon zest, cheese, and nutmeg, and cook until sauce has thickened and cheese has melted. Season with salt and pepper.

To Finish:

1 egg, beaten

1. Divide pasta dough into 4 portions and wrap the unused portions in plastic wrap to prevent drying. Using a pasta machine, roll dough into long sheets with the thinnest setting possible without the dough tearing.
2. Cut 2-inch circles of dough and place 1 teaspoon of artichoke/ricotta filling in center of dough. Brush perimeter of ravioli with egg wash and place another circle of dough over filling. Pinch tightly to seal seam. Place on flour-dusted sheet until ready to cook. Repeat until all the dough has been filled.
3. Cook ravioli in gently boiling salted water until tender, about 5 minutes. Drain and toss in Lemon and Parmesan-Cream Sauce. Serve immediately on warm plates.

green chile fest

– Menu –

- Green Chile Chicken Stew with Cheddar Cheese Biscuits •
- Green Chile Scalloped Potatoes • Green Chile Sopaipilla Stuffing •
- Green Chile, Apple, and Chicken Pot Pie • Green Chile Tortilla Pinwheels •
- Green Chile and Cheddar Polenta • Sautéed Spinach with Green Chiles •
- Lime Ice Cream with Caramelized Green Chile •

That famous question you are asked when dining in New Mexico: green chile or red chile? I love them both and love unraveling the mystery of cooking with chiles.

I'm always amazed at the age of the locals listed in the obituaries; most seem to be in their 80s and 90s. Could this long life come from eating chiles every day? Chiles are loaded with good things. One green chile has more vitamin C than an orange. All chiles lower cholesterol and blood pressure, are low in carbohydrates, and stimulate the endorphins in the brain that bring about a sense of well-being and happiness. What's not to love?

Once the green chile season hits, we offer this class regularly for visitors and locals alike. How wet the summer has been determines how hot the chiles will be. Chiles are affected by growing conditions in much the same way that grapes are.

Hatch chiles are New Mexico greens grown in the traditionally hotter and drier town of Hatch. Chimayo chiles come from the historic town of Chimayo and are New Mexico red chiles that develop from a ripened green.

Some chile names change once they are dried. A poblano becomes an ancho, and a jalapeño, when dried and smoked, becomes a chipotle. Fresh Anaheim chiles may be easily substituted for the fresh green New Mexico chiles in all of these recipes. •

facing: Blistering beauties

Green Chile Chicken Stew with Cheddar Cheese Biscuits

Chicken pot pie with a chile kick, made even better when topped with Cheddar Cheese Biscuits.

Serves 6

2 tablespoons butter

1 cup chopped onion

3 garlic cloves, minced

1-1/2 cups roasted, peeled, and chopped green chiles

3 tablespoons flour

1 tablespoon jalapeño pickle juice or white vinegar

3 cups chicken stock

1 teaspoon toasted and ground cumin seeds

1 teaspoon Mexican oregano, dried

1 teaspoon salt, or to taste

1/2 teaspoon freshly ground pepper

2 large red potatoes, diced into 1-inch cubes

1 1/2 cups poached chicken meat (legs, thighs, breasts, or combination)

1. Melt butter in a medium saucepan and sauté onion until soft and translucent.
2. Add garlic and allow to brown slightly. Stir in chiles.
3. Sprinkle flour over onion mixture, stir in, and let brown slightly.
4. Stir in pickle juice, stock, cumin, oregano, salt, pepper, and potatoes.
5. Reduce heat to simmer and cook about 10 minutes or until potatoes are almost tender. Stir in chicken.
6. Pour stew into a buttered 4-quart casserole dish and top with Cheddar Cheese Biscuits.

Green Chile Chicken Stew in the pot

Cheddar Cheese Biscuits

2 cups flour

1/2 teaspoon garlic powder

1/4 teaspoon black pepper

1/2 teaspoon salt

1/2 teaspoon ground red chile

4 teaspoons baking powder

8 tablespoons cold unsalted butter

1 cup shredded sharp Cheddar cheese

1 cup heavy cream, plus 2 teaspoons

1. In a medium bowl combine flour, garlic powder, pepper, salt, red chile, and baking powder.

2. Using a cheese grater, grate the butter into the flour and stir it until mixture resembles coarse meal.

3. Stir in the cheese. Add 1 cup cream and mix lightly with a wooden spoon until dough just holds together. Cover and let rest 10 minutes.

4. Using a large spoon, break off dollops of biscuits and drop onto surface of stew. Brush biscuit tops with remaining cream.

5. Bake stew, uncovered, in preheated 425-degree-F oven for 20 minutes or until biscuits are nicely brown.

Green chile fans

Green Chile Scalloped Potatoes

The quintessential comfort food that becomes something special and spicy with the addition of green chile. Try the red chile version in the Red Chile Fest chapter too!

Serves 6 to 8

4 medium potatoes, washed, peeled, and sliced very thin

1/4 cup butter

1/2 cup breadcrumbs

1-1/2 cups heavy cream

1-1/2 cups milk

1 teaspoon hot ground red chile

4 egg yolks, lightly beaten

1 cup shredded Monterey Jack or Cheddar cheese

1 teaspoon Mexican oregano

2 teaspoons salt

Freshly ground pepper

8 fresh green chiles, roasted, peeled, seeded, and chopped

1. Spread potatoes on paper towels and dry well.

2. Melt butter in a medium sauté pan and add breadcrumbs. Sauté crumbs until they are toasted and lightly browned. Remove from pan and set aside.

3. In a medium bowl, whisk together cream, milk, red chile, yolks, cheese, oregano, and salt.

4. Butter a 4-quart casserole dish. Scatter half of the potato slices over bottom of casserole. Crack freshly ground pepper over potatoes and scatter half of the green chiles over the top.

5. Pour half of the cream/egg mixture over potatoes. Add remaining potatoes and green chiles and pour remainder of milk/cream mixture over chiles. Top with toasted breadcrumbs.

6. Cover and bake at 400 degrees F for 40 minutes. Remove cover and continue baking 15 minutes more or until casserole is bubbling and nicely browned. Serve warm.

Green Chile Sopaipilla Stuffing

There always seems to be leftover sopaipillas when you dine in any of Santa Fe's great New Mexican restaurants. Take them home and make this tasty stuffing.

Serves 8 to 10

3 tablespoons butter

3/4 cup diced onion

2 garlic cloves, minced

2 yellow squash, roughly chopped

2 zucchini, roughly chopped

6 fresh green chiles, roasted and peeled, or 3/4 cup chopped canned green chiles

2 jalapeños, minced

1 teaspoon toasted and ground cumin seed

1 teaspoon Mexican oregano

1 teaspoon kosher salt

1-1/2 cups chicken broth

6 large sopaipillas*

1/2 cup toasted pine nuts

1. Melt butter in medium saucepan and sauté onion until soft. Add garlic, squash, and zucchini, and sauté until vegetables start to brown slightly. Slice chiles into 1-inch square pieces and stir into mixture. Add jalapeños.
2. Add spices and salt. Stir in chicken broth and set aside.
3. Tear sopaipillas into 1-inch pieces and place in large bowl. Add vegetables and pine nuts, and mix well.
4. Place stuffing in well-buttered 3-quart casserole and bake at 375 degrees F for 30 minutes or until stuffing is nicely brown.

* Sopaipillas are a local bread similar to the beignets of New Orleans. If they are not available in your area, you can find a recipe in many Southwest cookbooks. Twelve slices of any white bread may be substituted as well.

Green Chile, Apple, and Chicken Pot Pie

Makes 8 small pies

4 tablespoons butter, divided, plus additional for ramekins

1/4 cup minced celery

1/2 cup minced onion

1 Granny Smith apple, cored and finely chopped

1/4 cup chopped, roasted green chile

2 tablespoons dry vermouth or dry white wine

1 teaspoon lemon juice

1 teaspoon chopped fresh parsley

1/2 teaspoon chopped fresh thyme

Salt and pepper, to taste

2 chicken breasts, trimmed and cut into 1-inch cubes

1/2 cup grated sharp Cheddar cheese

2 eggs, beaten

1 batch Real Flaky Pie Crust (page 19)

Chef Chat—
Oyster lovers take note. In a class I call Oyster Lovers Unite, we make a version of this recipe substituting raw oyster in place of the chicken. Place three shucked raw oysters in each ramekin and top with the green chile and apple mixture. Top with cheese and crust. Twenty minutes is all it takes to cook the oysters perfectly. Yum!

1. Butter eight 6-ounce ramekins and place in refrigerator.

2. Melt 2 tablespoons butter over medium heat in a large skillet and sauté celery, onion, and apple until tender, about 5 minutes.

3. Add chile, vermouth, lemon juice, parsley, and thyme, and sauté for 1 minute. Remove from heat and season with salt and pepper.

4. Melt remaining butter in a sauté pan and cook chicken until it is almost cooked through. Divide chicken among the ramekins, top with green chile and apple mixture, and sprinkle with Cheddar cheese. Brush egg onto rim of each ramekin.

5. Roll out pie crust to 1/8 inch thickness and cut circles of dough 1/4 inch larger than ramekins.

6. Place dough over each ramekin and pinch down to seal. Cut 2 steam vents in crust and brush tops with beaten egg.

7. Bake at 375 degrees F for 20 minutes or until crust is nicely browned. Serve hot.

facing: Fill, crimp, glaze, bake

Green Chile Tortilla Pinwheels

These pretty pinwheels can be made ahead and sliced just before you serve them.

Serves 10 to 12

8 ounces cream cheese

1 tablespoon fresh lime juice

2 shallots, minced

1/2 teaspoon salt

1/2 teaspoon white pepper

2 fresh New Mexico green chiles, roasted, peeled, seeded, and finely chopped, or 1/4 cup canned chopped green chiles, drained of juice

1 tablespoon chopped cilantro

4 (10-inch) flour tortillas

1. In a small mixing bowl, mash together cream cheese, lime juice, shallots, salt, pepper, chiles, and cilantro with a fork.
2. Warm tortillas in microwave for 10 seconds to soften; allow to cool.
3. Spread one-fourth of the cream cheese mixture over entire surface of each tortilla. Starting on one side, roll up as tightly as possible.
4. Wrap tortillas in plastic wrap and refrigerate for 30 minutes or until service time.
5. Unwrap tortillas and slice into 1/2-inch pinwheels, turn on their sides, garnish with additional leaves of cilantro, and serve.

above: Green Chile and Cheddar Polenta with Pecan- and Herb-Crusted Salmon

Green Chile and Cheddar Polenta

These are really just cheesy grits with green chile. Polenta sounds fancier!

Serves 4 to 6

2 tablespoons unsalted butter

1 teaspoon minced shallots

1 teaspoon minced garlic

3 cups half-and-half

1-1/2 cups chicken stock

1 teaspoon Mexican oregano

1/4 teaspoon freshly ground pepper

1 cup yellow cornmeal

1 cup grated sharp Cheddar cheese

8 fresh green chiles, roasted, peeled, seeded, and diced in
 1/4-inch pieces, or 1 cup canned chopped chiles

1. Melt the butter over medium-low heat in a 5-quart, heavy-bottomed saucepot. Add the shallots and garlic, and cook for about 1 minute, until the shallots are translucent, taking care not to brown the butter.
2. Add the half-and-half, stock, oregano, and pepper, and increase the heat to medium.
3. Simmer for 3 minutes at a low boil.
4. Whisking constantly, slowly pour the cornmeal into the simmering stock. Decrease the heat and continue to cook, stirring constantly with a wooden spoon for about 5 minutes, until the polenta thickens and pulls away from the sides of the pot.
5. Remove from heat and fold in the cheese and chiles. Serve warm.

Alternate Serving Style:

1. While the polenta is still warm, pour it into a buttered jellyroll pan. With a spatula lightly rubbed with oil to prevent it from sticking, smooth the surface until polenta is flat and even. Let cool for 15 minutes, then cover tightly with plastic wrap, and set in refrigerator for about 1 hour, until it is firm to the touch.
2. Remove the polenta from the refrigerator. With a 3-inch cookie cutter, cut six circles out of the polenta and set aside. Warm the circles in a 350-degree-F oven. Reserve the remainder of the polenta for another use.

Sautéed Spinach with Green Chiles

Maybe if there had been chiles sautéed into the spinach I was served as a kid I would have loved it then as much as I do now.

Serves 4

2 tablespoons butter

1 tablespoon olive oil

1 teaspoon minced garlic

4 fresh New Mexico green chiles, roasted, peeled, seeded, and chopped, or 1/2 cup canned chopped green chiles

1 tablespoon dry vermouth

2 pounds spinach, washed and dried

Kosher salt and freshly ground pepper, to taste

1. Melt butter in large saucepan. Add olive oil and garlic, and cook until garlic is slightly browned.
2. Add chiles and sauté briefly.
3. Add vermouth and spinach. Cover pan and allow to steam for 3 minutes.
4. Uncover pan and stir spinach to combine with chiles. Season with salt and pepper, drain liquid, and serve at once.

Lime Ice Cream with Caramelized Green Chile

This tart lime ice cream will pucker you up. Wait till you feel the heat of the caramelized green chile!
Makes about 1-1/2 quarts

Lime Ice Cream

> 2 cups heavy cream
> 1 cup milk
> 1 cup sugar
> Zest of 2 limes
> 1/4 cup freshly squeezed lime juice
> 1/4 cup key lime juice (bottled is fine)

1. Whisk together cream, milk, sugar, and zest; mix until sugar is completely dissolved.
2. Quickly stir in lime juices and pour into ice cream maker.
3. Freeze according to manufacturer's instructions.

Caramelized Green Chile

> 6 fresh New Mexico green chiles, roasted, peeled, seeded, and rinsed
> 1/2 cup sugar
> 2 tablespoons water
> 1/4 teaspoon salt

Chef Chat—
It sounds crazy but these candied chiles end up tasting like candied pineapple, with a kick. If you are not sure you will love them, serve them on top of the ice cream.

1. Blot chiles dry with paper towels and cut them into 1/4-inch strips.
2. Combine all ingredients in heavy-bottomed saucepan.
3. Cook over medium heat, stirring occasionally until mixture thickens and becomes syrupy, about 12 minutes.
4. Remove from heat and strain chiles through a sieve. Scatter chiles on lightly oiled plate and freeze. Stir into Lime Ice Cream before storing ice cream in freezer.

facing: New Mexico bounty

red chile fest

– Menu –

- Red Chile Pork Tamales -
- Vegetarian Yam Tamales -
- Eggplant Adovado -
- Red Chile Scalloped Potatoes -
- Red Chile Cauliflower -
- Dulce de Leche Ice Cream with Red Chile Caramel Sauce -
- Red Chile Caramel Sauce -

No icon is more associated with New Mexico than the glorious chile ristra—the brilliantly red, hanging bunches of dried New Mexico chiles. As ornamental as they are, realize that many locals actually cook with the tasty pods; the tradition of stringing them was originally done to preserve this important ingredient for use during the winter months.

If you visit us and take a ristra home, be sure they have not been sprayed with pesticides or shellacked before you set about cooking with them. I prefer to cook with pure ground red chile, which differs vastly from the "chile powder" we grew up with, which includes many other ingredients—preservatives, salt, and spices—and is no substitute for the pure version.

One question students often ask is "which is hotter, green or red?" As the chile ripens from green to red, the naturally occurring sugars in the flesh develop and can tame the heat slightly. Realize, though, that the more seeds that are added in the grinding process, the hotter the ground powder will be. If you purchase the chile in bulk and it is not labeled either hot

facing: Ruby red chile sauce

or mild, generally speaking the deeper red or more magenta the color is, the milder it will be. If it is more orange and bright, you can guess that it will be hot. The best test is to lick your finger, dip it into the powder, and then place it on the tip of your tongue . . . you will know right away what you got!

Any of the recipes in this chapter can be tamed for piquancy simply by substituting all or part of the hot chile with mild. I love a kick in my chile dishes, but not so hot that smoke shoots out of my ears and my taste buds go numb. After cooking from this chapter and the Green Chile Fest chapter, it's your turn to decide, green or red? If you can't decide, you join a rapidly growing group of chile lovers that belong to the "Christmas" lovers club—you love both green and red chiles on the same plate. •

Red Chile Pork Tamales

There are references to the making of tamales recorded in the human culinary history going as far back as 5000 B.C. Once served primarily for special occasions, now tamales are enjoyed year-round. The wrapping technique is tricky; but once you get it down, you'll be whipping them up in a breeze. Invite friends and family to join in making them—it's more fun in a group.

Serves 10 (4 to 5 small tamales each)

40 to 50 dried corn husks
Red Chile Pork Filling (below)

Masa Mixture (see page 118)
Red Chile Sauce (see page 167)

For the Husks:

1. Place the husks in a large deep bowl and cover with hot water. Place a plate on the husks so that they are submerged in the water. Allow to soften for 20 minutes. When soft, separate the husks and remove any corn silk. Keep in the water as you make the tamales.

Red Chile Pork Filling

1 1/2 pounds boneless pork shoulder, butt, or top sirloin
2 cups chicken stock
2 tablespoons lard
2 garlic cloves, minced

1/2 cup ground hot red chile
1 teaspoon salt
1 teaspoon Mexican oregano
1/2 teaspoon ground cumin

1. Cut the pork into 1-inch cubes and remove any connective tissue. Place meat in a medium saucepan and cover with chicken stock. Simmer for 20 minutes or until pork is cooked through.
2. Remove the meat from the stock, reserving the stock. Chop meat into very small pieces. Heat lard in a frying pan and sauté chopped meat until browned. Add garlic and cook 2 more minutes.
3. Remove from heat and add chile, salt, oregano, and cumin.
4. Return pan to heat and add enough reserved stock to create a moist-but-not-runny filling. Simmer for 5 minutes. Remove from heat and allow to cool to room temperature before stuffing tamales.

facing: New Mexico icon—the chile ristra

Masa Mixture

2 tablespoons ground mild red chile

6 cups masa

4 to 5 cups warm water, including remainder of pork stock

2 cups cold lard

2 teaspoons salt

1. In a large bowl, stir chile into masa and add enough water to make a moist dough similar in consistency to a thick oatmeal.
2. In a medium bowl, whip the lard with the salt until very fluffy and light enough to float on the surface of cold water.
3. Fold the whipped lard into the masa mixture, making sure it is completely incorporated. Do not overmix.

Assembling the Tamales:

1. Make some tamale ties by tearing strips 1/8 inch wide from a few of the husks. Take one husk and open it with the narrow end away from you. Spread a 3 x 3-inch square of masa 1 inch from the bottom.
2. Take 1/2 teaspoon of the filling and place it in a narrow strip going from the bottom of the tamale toward the top, 1/4 inch wide. Resist the temptation to overfill the tamale.
3. Roll the husk over the masa to completely cover the filling. Fold the bottom of the tamale up and twist the top. Tie both top and bottom of tamale with husk ties.

Cooking the Tamales:

1. Place tamales vertically into a steamer. Add 3 inches of water to the pan. Place a penny in the bottom of the pan— this will rattle and warn you if you are running out of water during the steaming time.
2. Steam the tamales over boiling water for 45 minutes or until masa is set up and tamales lose their shiny look. Serve hot with Red Chile Sauce (see page 167).

Vegetarian Yam Tamales

Vegetarians get nervous when talking about dishes traditionally prepared with lard. This version I developed for folks who don't "do" animal products.

6 cups masa	2 cups baked yam purée
2 teaspoons salt	1/4 cup extra virgin olive oil
Approximately 5 cups warm water	1/4 pound Monterey Jack cheese
60 to 70 dried corn husks	4 poblano chiles, roasted and peeled

1. In a large bowl, mix masa, salt, and water, adding just enough water to form a wet masa mixture.
2. Soak cornhusks in hot water to soften.
3. With electric mixer, whip yam purée and olive oil until light and fluffy.
4. Gently fold masa into yam purée to combine.
5. Cut cheese into matchstick-size pieces. Cut poblanos into thin strips, about 1/4 inch wide.

Assembling the Tamales:

1. Make some tamale ties by tearing strips 1/8 inch wide from a few of the husks. Take one husk and open it with the narrow end away from you. Spread a 3 x 3-inch square of masa one inch from the bottom.
2. Take 1 piece of cheese and 1 strip of poblano and place them side by side in a narrow strip going from the bottom of the tamale toward the top.
3. Roll the husk over the masa to completely cover the cheese and chile. Fold the bottom of the tamale up and twist the top. Tie both top and bottom of tamale with husk ties.

Cooking the Tamales:

1. Place tamales vertically into a steamer. Add 3 inches of water to the pan. Place a penny in the bottom of the pan; it will rattle and warn you if you are running out of water during the steaming time.
2. Steam the tamales over boiling water for 30 minutes or until masa is set up and tamales lose their shiny look. Serve hot with Red Chile Sauce (see page 167).

Eggplant Adovado

Red chile is too good to use only with meat. This eggplant version of a classic meat marinade will fool everyone into thinking they are savoring beef or pork—especially if used in a burrito or as a filling for tacos.

Serves 6 as a side dish

3 cups diced eggplant

3 cups vegetable oil

1/4 cup crushed caribe chile

2 tablespoons ground mild red chile

2 tablespoons ground hot red chile

4 garlic cloves, crushed

1 tablespoon toasted and ground cumin

1 teaspoon Mexican oregano

1-1/2 teaspoons salt

Juice of 1 lime

2 cups water

Garnishes—grated Cheddar cheese, sour cream, cilantro

Chef Chat—
Use this as the filling for vegetarian tacos, taquitos, or tamales. The cooked-down eggplant will taste like a delicious sweet meat filling.

1. Peel and dice eggplant into 2-inch cubes. Place in colander and allow to drain for 20 minutes.
2. Heat vegetable oil in a large saucepan; when very hot, fry eggplant until golden brown.
3. Drain eggplant on paper towels.
4. Place chiles, garlic, cumin, oregano, salt, lime juice, and water in a blender and blend until smooth.
5. Scatter eggplant in large baking dish and pour chile mixture over it. Stir and allow to marinate for 10 minutes.
6. Cover dish and bake at 400 degrees F for 30 minutes or until sauce has thickened and coated eggplant. Serve with grated Cheddar cheese, sour cream, and sprigs of fresh cilantro.

Red Chile Scalloped Potatoes

These potatoes are rich and creamy and loaded with the fabulous flavor of New Mexico red chile. Serve with roast pork or ham to give them a kick.

Serves 6 to 8

3 medium potatoes, washed, peeled, and sliced very thin

4 egg yolks, lightly beaten

1 cup heavy cream

2 cups milk

1 cup sour cream

1 cup shredded sharp Cheddar cheese

1 teaspoon ground hot red chile

1/4 cup ground mild red chile

1 teaspoon toasted and ground cumin

1-1/2 teaspoons salt

Freshly ground pepper

1. Spread potatoes on paper towels and dry well.
2. In a medium bowl, whisk together yolks, cream, milk, sour cream, cheese, chiles, cumin, and salt.
3. Butter a 4-quart casserole dish. Place potatoes in a large bowl and pour milk/cream mixture over them. Stir to completely coat potatoes.
4. Place potatoes in a casserole and crack freshly ground pepper over top.
5. Cover and bake at 400 degrees F for 30 minutes. Uncover and continue baking until potatoes are tender and casserole is bubbling and nicely browned, about 20 minutes.

facing: Garlic and onions

Red Chile Cauliflower

More great red chile comfort food—and low carb to boot!

Serves 6 as a side dish

1/4 cup crushed caribe chile

2 teaspoons ground mild red chile

2 tablespoons ground hot red chile

3 garlic cloves, crushed

1 tablespoon toasted and ground cumin

1 teaspoon Mexican oregano

1 teaspoon salt

2 cups vegetable stock

3 cups cauliflower florets

1. Place chiles, garlic, cumin, oregano, salt, and stock in a blender and blend until smooth.

2. Scatter cauliflower in large baking dish and pour chile mixture over it. Allow to marinate for 10 minutes.

3. Bake uncovered at 375 degrees F for 45 minutes or until sauce has thickened and coated cauliflower.

Dulce de Leche Ice Cream with
Red Chile Caramel Sauce

The true flavor of dulce de leche comes from sugar and goat's milk. Here I hint at that effect by substituting brown sugar for white.

Makes 1-1/2 quarts

2 cups heavy cream
1 cup whole milk
1 cup brown sugar, divided
1 teaspoon vanilla
6 large egg yolks

1. In a heavy medium saucepan, bring the cream, milk, 1/2 cup brown sugar, and vanilla to a simmer over low heat. Stir to dissolve sugar. Remove from heat.
2. Whisk egg yolks with remaining brown sugar in a medium bowl until glossy and light.
3. Whisk 1/4 cup of the hot milk mixture into yolks. Gradually whisk remaining milk into egg mixture. Return mixture to low heat and simmer, stirring constantly, until custard is thick enough to coat the back of a wooden spoon (about 8 to 10 minutes).
4. Strain custard into a metal bowl and chill submerged in ice water until completely cold, or cover and refrigerate overnight. Transfer custard to ice cream machine and freeze according to manufacturer's directions. Once ice cream has reached the appropriate texture, transfer to a glass or plastic bowl, cover, and freeze. Serve with Red Chile Caramel Sauce (see page 127).

Red Chile Caramel Sauce

I need to bottle this sweet and spicy sauce. In the meantime, you can make it at home. I love to throw taste buds off-kilter and surprise the palate. Drizzle this sauce over the Dulce de Leche Ice Cream and top with toasted pine nuts for a real treat.

Makes 1-1/2 cups

1/3 cup water

1 cup sugar

1 cup heavy cream

1 teaspoon salt

2 tablespoons ground hot red chile, or to taste

1. Place water and sugar in a heavy saucepan and stir to moisten sugar. Bring to a boil.
2. Using a pastry brush repeatedly dipped in cold water, keep side of pan free of sugar crystals. Allow mixture to boil until it reaches a deep golden brown color, about 15 minutes.
3. Remove from heat and carefully stir in cream using a long-handled wooden spoon, as mixture will bubble up and could burn you.
4. Return to heat and cook until caramel becomes smooth; stir in salt. Allow to cool, stir in chile, cover, and refrigerate for up to 2 weeks.

facing: Red Chile Caramel Sauce swirl
above: Swirling the sauce

bbq bravado

THRILLING GRILLING

– *Menu* –

• Blue Corn Muffins •

• Tandoori Chicken Wings •

• Cuban-Style Barbecue Pork •

• Low-Carb-Be-Que Sauce •

• Smoked Tomato and Chipotle Barbecue Sauce •

• Caramelized Onion Barbecue Sauce •

• Smoked Potato Salad •

• Asian Coleslaw •

• Classic Strawberry Shortcake •

Many parts of New Mexico are blessed with almost nine months of outdoor grilling weather. Homes that have covered portals allow the firing up of the grill even on sunny winter days. Wherever you live, food cooked over wood, charcoal, or even lava stones takes on an extra smoky layer of flavor; we all love it. Throughout the summer months, I offer a wide variety of grilling classes covering a wide span of topics: Hot off the Asian Grill, Tapas on the Grill, Mediterranean Grilling, I Wish I Knew How to Grill Fish. My favorite is a good ol'-fashioned American grilling class. This menu is reminiscent of my youth in Rochester, but with a gourmet spin. Sometimes I call this class Thrilling Grilling; either way it's time to head out to the BBQ. •

facing: Ribs hot on the grill

Blue Corn Muffins

There are great to serve with grilled meat. Look for blue corn flour in the Mexican food section of your grocery store. Yellow cornmeal will work too, but I love the blue tint the blue corn flour gives these rich muffins.

Makes 18 muffins

3/4 cup butter

1/2 cup cream cheese

1/3 cup sugar

4 eggs

1/2 cup buttermilk

2 jalapeños, seeded and minced

1 cup drained canned corn

3/4 cup grated sharp Cheddar cheese

1 cup flour

1 cup blue corn flour

2 1/2 teaspoons baking powder

1 teaspoon salt

1. Preheat oven to 375 degrees F. Arrange cupcake papers in pans. Cream together the butter, cream cheese, and sugar with an electric mixer in a large bowl.

2. Add eggs, buttermilk, jalapeños, corn, and cheese, mixing after each ingredient addition.

3. Sift together dry ingredients into a medium bowl. Add dry mixture to batter in three batches, mixing after each addition. Spoon the batter into muffin tins.

4. Bake for 20 minutes or until a toothpick comes out clean when inserted into center of muffins. Serve warm with butter and honey.

Chef Chat—
A large ice cream scoop is an accurate way to divide the batter between the cups. These muffins freeze well and stay moist due to all that wonderful fat: buttermilk, cream cheese, and Cheddar. Remember: fat is flavor!

Tandoori Chicken Wings

Great curry flavor without the need of a tandoori oven in the kitchen.

Serves 6 (6 each)

36 chicken wing drummettes

3 cups canned chicken stock

1-1/2 cups whole-milk yogurt

Juice of 1 lemon

2 tablespoons garam masala, available from Asian
   and East Indian markets

1 teaspoon kosher salt

1/2 cup chopped fresh cilantro

1. Place the chicken wings in a large pot and pour the
   stock over them. Bring to a boil and reduce heat to
   a simmer; poach wings for 10 minutes. Drain and
   set aside.

2. Meanwhile mix yogurt, lemon juice, garam masala,
   and salt in a large bowl.

3. Add wings to yogurt mix, toss, and allow them to
   marinate for at least 1 hour.

4. Prepare the grill and remove wings from the yogurt.
   Take remaining marinade and place in a small
   saucepan. Bring to a boil and serve hot as a dipping
   sauce.

5. Grill wings, turning occasionally until lightly
   charred and crispy. Scatter cilantro over wings and
   serve immediately.

Chef Chat—
*Garam masala is a spicy curry powder–like
spice blend. Garam means hot and masala
means a mix of spices.*

above: Grilling wings

Cuban-Style Barbecue Pork

This recipe is inspired by a marinade used for whole roast suckling pig—Cuban style. The Cubans and Miamians use a sour orange as the juice in this dish. A mix of lime and orange juice is a good substitute and gives the pork a tart citrus kick.

Serves 6

Juice of 3 oranges

Juice of 2 limes

6 garlic cloves, minced

1/2 cup chopped fresh oregano leaves

2 teaspoons kosher salt

2 pounds boneless pork loin

1. Combine citrus juices, garlic, oregano, and salt in a mixing bowl.
2. Tenderize meat* and place in shallow pan.
3. Pour marinade over meat, turn once, and cover. Allow meat to marinate for at least 1 hour and up to 12 hours refrigerated.
4. Prepare the grill and grill meat over hot coals until meat thermometer reaches 140 degrees F.
5. Slice and serve with Lime-Garlic Mojo (see below).

*Gadget Gab—Tenderize the meat with a Jaccard meat tenderizer. The pork will drink up the marinade, and cooking time will be decreased by one-third.

Lime-Garlic Mojo

Juice of 1 lime

Juice of 1 orange

2 garlic cloves, minced

1 teaspoon fresh oregano leaves

1 teaspoon toasted and ground cumin seeds

1/2 teaspoon salt

1/3 cup extra virgin olive oil

1. Combine citrus juices, garlic, oregano, cumin, and salt in a medium bowl.
2. Slowly whisk in olive oil. Cover and refrigerate until serving.

Low-Carb-Be-Que Sauce

When the Atkins Diet craze hit, I was offering a low-carb class of some kind once every two weeks and they always sold out. Now there are many versions of this popular diet (and it's considered good health to cut back on sugars in any diet). This BBQ sauce is delicious regardless of your dietary plan. This sauce has 2 carbs for every 2 tablespoons.

Yields about 3 cups

1/4 cup olive oil

2 garlic cloves, minced

6 scallions, chopped fine, tops and root ends discarded

4 tablespoons Splenda granular, or 4 packets
    artificial sweetener

1 teaspoon salt

2 teaspoons dry mustard

1-1/2 teaspoons smoked Spanish paprika

1 teaspoon hot New Mexico red chile powder

1/2 teaspoon freshly ground black pepper

1 tablespoon molasses

1-1/2 cups water

1/4 cup cider vinegar

2 tablespoons Worcestershire sauce

1 (6-ounce) can tomato paste

1 tablespoon liquid smoke (optional)

1. Place oil in a medium saucepan and sauté garlic and scallions until slightly browned.
2. Stir in Splenda, salt, mustard, paprika, red chile, pepper, molasses, water, vinegar, and Worcestershire sauce. Stir to combine. Simmer for 15 minutes over low heat.
3. Whisk in tomato paste and liquid smoke, if using, and simmer another 10 minutes.
4. Let the mixture cool and transfer to a jar with a tight-fitting lid. Sauce will last 1 week in refrigerator.

above: Goodies for the sauce

Smoked Pot[...]

Heck, I'll even smoke potatoes. This is one of the La[...] many grilled dishes.

Serves 6 to 8

4 cups new potatoes, quartered

3/4 cup finely diced celery

1/2 cup finely diced red bell pepper

1/2 cup finely diced yellow bell pepper

1/4 cup finely diced green bell pepper

1/2 cup chopped scallions, tops and root
ends discarded

2 teaspoons freshly squeezed lime juice

1 teaspoon salt

1 teaspoon freshly ground pepper

1 teaspoon smoked Spanish paprika

3/4 cup mayonnaise, or to taste

1. Cover potatoes with cold salted water in large
   saucepan and bring to a boil. Cook potatoes until
   fork tender. Drain and immediately smoke for 10
   minutes, using the mildest wood available, such as
   alder, cherry, or apple.

2. Remove potatoes from the smoker and allow to cool.

3. Meanwhile in a medium bowl, mix celery, bell peppers, scallions, lime juice, salt, pepper, and paprika.

4. Add potatoes and mayonnaise; toss well. Allow salad
   to sit refrigerated for at least 1/2 hour for flavors to
   meld. Garnish with a sprinkle of additional smoked
   Spanish paprika and serve.

above: Cooked new potatoes

Smoked Tomato and Chipotle Barbecue Sauce

Smoking the tomatoes before adding them to the sauce gives a wonderful extra bit of smokiness to whatever you spread this on. The chipotles help too.

Makes about 3 cups

15 Roma tomatoes, halved and smoked for 10 minutes over mild wood

1/4 cup olive oil

1/2 cup cider vinegar

2 teaspoons lemon juice

1/2 cup brown sugar

1/4 cup Worcestershire sauce

2 teaspoons chipotles in adobo, or to taste

1/2 cup molasses

2 teaspoons dry mustard

1 teaspoon kosher salt

1 teaspoon smoked Spanish paprika

1/2 cup water

1. Peel and finely chop smoked tomatoes. Whisk together the remaining ingredients in a medium saucepan and
   stir in tomatoes.

2. Cook over medium heat for 20 minutes and allow the sauce to thicken.

3. Marinate meat in sauce 1 hour before grilling and continually baste while grilling.

Caramelized Oni[...]

Sweet caramelized onions add another dimension [...]

Makes about 3 cups

1 large onion, thinly sliced
2 teaspoons balsamic vinegar
2 teaspoons plus 1/4 cup brown sugar
1-1/2 cups ketchup
1/4 cup olive oil
1/4 cup cider vinegar

1. Place onion in a heavy, dry skillet and sauté over medi[...]
   the heat and add balsamic vinegar and 2 teaspoons bro[...]
   simmer for 10 minutes and remove from heat.
2. Whisk together remaining ingredients in a medium sau[...]
   sauce will start to thicken.
3. Finely chop caramelized onions and stir into barbecue [...]
4. Marinate meat in sauce for 1 hour before grilling and [...]

above: Recipe files

Asian Coleslaw

This is a nice change from the mayonnaise-based slaws of my youth. I love the crunch the fried shallots and peanuts give this spicy side dish. It's a great salad for a barbecue.

Serves 8 to 10

1 cup white vinegar
1/2 cup sugar
2 teaspoons salt
2 cucumbers, cut into julienne
2 cups sliced red cabbage
2 cups sliced green cabbage
1 carrot, cut into julienne
6 Thai chiles, chopped, or to taste
1/2 cup roughly chopped cilantro
1/2 cup chopped peanuts
1/4 cup fried shallots, available in Asian markets

1. Mix together vinegar, sugar, and salt in a small glass bowl. Set aside.
2. In a large bowl, toss together cucumber, cabbage, carrot, chiles, and cilantro. Pour vinegar mixture over vegetables and toss well.
3. Cover and refrigerate for up to one hour. Stir occasionally.
4. When ready to serve, top with peanuts and fried shallots.

Chef Chat—
A mandolin makes cutting cucumbers and cabbages so easy.
It's a good idea to wear rubber gloves when chopping Thai chiles—
they're hot!

Chef Chat—
Perfecting delicate biscuits is one of the fundamentals of baking I like to teach beginning cooks. Remember biscuits, pie crusts, and scones are shortbread, meaning the less you mix them, the more tender they will be. However, the dough should not be dry and crumbly, so knead enough to hold it together. Biscuits are not like cookie dough in that it's not a good idea to reroll the dough after cutting. Try to cut biscuits as close together as you can!

Classic Strawberry Shortcake

What dish better represents summer? Make this stunning dessert when the strawberries are fat, juicy, and full of flavor. A perfect dessert for an outdoor picnic.

Serves 6

For the Shortcake:

2 cups all-purpose flour

2 1/4 teaspoons baking powder

1/4 teaspoon baking soda

1/2 teaspoon salt

2 tablespoons sugar

1/3 cup cold unsalted butter

3/4 cup cold buttermilk, plus 2 tablespoons

1. Preheat oven to 450 degrees F. Make the biscuits by combining all dry ingredients in a medium mixing bowl.
2. Using a cheese grater, grate the butter and blend into dry ingredients using 2 butter knives or a pastry blender.
3. Slowly stir in buttermilk and mix dough just until it holds together.
4. Turn dough onto a lightly floured board and knead gently until a cohesive ball forms.
5. Pat down dough and lightly flour surface. Roll dough to 1-1/2 inches thick.
6. Using a 3-inch biscuit cutter, cut biscuits as close together as possible.
7. Place biscuits on an ungreased baking sheet. Bake for 12 to 15 minutes, until nicely browned.

To Assemble:

1-1/2 cups heavy cream whipped with 3 tablespoons confectioners' sugar and 1 teaspoon vanilla

3 cups sliced strawberries marinated in 2 tablespoons Triple Sec liqueur

Powdered sugar

Fresh mint

1. Place 1 biscuit in each of six serving bowls. Slice biscuits in half along the equator and remove the top. Place 1 heaping tablespoon of whipped cream on each biscuit bottom.
2. Scatter 2 heaping tablespoons of strawberries onto whipped cream. Top with second slice of biscuit and then more whipped cream and finish with more berries. Garnish with a light dusting of powdered sugar and a sprig of fresh mint.

fab fajitas & sexy salsas

PARTY UNDER THE PORTAL

– Menu –

· Chile Con Queso · Homemade Flour Tortillas · Great Guacamole ·

· Pico de Gallo · Grilled Corn and Pinto Bean Salsa · Lime Chicken Fajitas ·

· Jerked Pork Fajitas · Cilantro-Grilled Flank Steak Fajitas ·

· Fajita Fixin's · Chocolate Pine Nut Tacos ·

T ender, tasty marinated meats off the grill and a variety of zippy salsas are a great way to throw together a party that can be prepared mostly in advance.

When spring arrives we New Mexicans joyously head to the backyard and to the barbecue, ready to begin a season of outdoor cooking. No matter where you live, outdoor entertaining gets us out of the kitchen and into the fresh air.

Planning a party "alfresco" requires some forethought, but once the foods for the grill are marinating, the preparation of a few salads, salsas, and side dishes are all that's required of an organized host or hostess. Make it your goal to have everything ready to pull out of the fridge once your guests arrive, so that you get to enjoy the party too.

Fajitas originated with the Mexican rancheros who worked the cattle ranches in Texas and were given the unpopular flank steak cuts to eat. The rancheros knew that by pounding the meat to tenderize it and marinating it in garlic and lime, the acid of the lime juice not only flavored the beef but also broke down the tough sinewy tissue and tenderized it. Now a popular restaurant dish and party food, flank steak has skyrocketed in price and may be harder to find. Ask your butcher for it and don't forget to grill extra vegetables for the vegetarians in the group.

Prepare the guacamole and salsa in the morning and have them already in their serving bowls, wrapped in plastic wrap along with the grated cheese, sour cream, and cut-up limes, ready to serve. Watch for interesting serving plates, platters, and bowls on sale at kitchen stores. Three of my favorite colorful serving bowls came from a discount closeout store and cost one dollar each. ·

facing: Fajita fixin's

Chile con Queso

Chile con Queso, meaning "chile with cheese," is naturally low carb, and it's a wonderful dip to enjoy with crisp low-carb veggies or healthy baked tortilla chips. It freezes well and doesn't separate when left over a flame on the buffet or picnic table. Use a fondue pot with a candle under it and dig in for an appetizer while grilling and enjoying the great outdoors. Thanks to Chef Kevin Weinberg, who worked for me in Sydney years ago, for this recipe.

Serves 12 people as a dip

2 tablespoons unsalted butter

6 fresh green chiles, roasted, peeled, seeded and chopped into 1/4-inch pieces, or 1 cup canned, diced green chiles

4 jalapeños, seeded and finely diced

1 medium onion, finely chopped

3 cloves garlic, minced

1 tablespoon toasted and ground cumin seed

1 tablespoon freshly ground pepper

3 tablespoons flour

1 cup vegetable stock

1 cup cream

3 cups grated sharp Cheddar cheese

1 cup grated Parmesan cheese

8 ounces cream cheese, cut into 1-inch chunks

1 tablespoon kosher salt

2 tablespoons white tequila

2 Roma tomatoes, diced

1. Melt the butter in a heavy-bottomed, medium saucepan over low heat. Add chiles, jalapeños, onion, and garlic, and sauté over medium heat until onions brown slightly.

2. Add the cumin, pepper, and flour, and stir until completely blended. Stir in the stock and cream, and reduce heat to low. Simmer gently for 10 minutes.

3. Add the cheeses all at once and stir until melted and mixture is smooth. Add the salt, tequila, and tomatoes, and stir to combine. Transfer to chafing dish or fondue pot and serve hot with jicama strips, bell pepper fingers, cauliflower florets, or corn chips.

Homemade Flour Tortillas

Imagine how impressed your guests will be if you make your own tortillas. (Your favorite brand of store-bought tortillas will work too.)

Makes 12 8-inch tortillas

3 cups flour

1 cup whole wheat flour

2 teaspoons baking powder

1 teaspoon salt

1 teaspoon sugar

1/4 cup lard or non-trans fat vegetable shortening, chilled

1-1/2 cups warm (not hot) water

1. Mix dry ingredients in a medium bowl. Break up lard or shortening into small pieces with your fingers and rub it into the flour mixture, combining until it resembles coarse meal.

2. Add the water, a little at a time, until a soft and manageable dough forms. Knead for 3 minutes and allow dough to rest, covered for 20 minutes.

3. Divide dough into 12 golfball-size balls. Roll out each ball on a well-floured board to create an 8-inch circle, 1/8 inch thick.

4. Cook each tortilla on a lightly oiled griddle, adding a small amount of oil each time, for 1 to 2 minutes on each side, or until small brown spots appear.

5. Cover and keep tortillas warm until service. To freeze: separate each cooled tortilla with waxed paper and place in a large ziplock bag.

above: **Toasty tortilla**

Great Guacamole

The buttery rich flavor of avocados and the natural health benefits from eating them make this recipe a must to have on hand. Everything about avocados is great: vitamin E, potassium, magnesium, fiber, and those heart-healthy monounsaturated fats. Hence the name Great Guacamole.

Makes 2 cups

2 ripe Hass avocados

2 teaspoons fresh lime juice

1/2 teaspoon kosher salt

2 garlic cloves, minced

1 Roma tomato, finely diced

1/4 cup finely chopped onion

2 scallions, white and green parts finely chopped, root ends discarded

1 large jalapeño, minced

3 tablespoons stemmed and chopped fresh cilantro

1. Halve and pit avocados. Scoop out flesh into medium bowl. Using 2 dinner knives, crosscut avocados into small 1/4-inch pieces.

2. Add lime juice, salt, and garlic, and mix slightly. Fold in tomato, onion, scallions, jalapeño, and cilantro. Cover guacamole with plastic wrap, pressing it right onto the surface of the guacamole; refrigerate. This will keep it from browning for up to 3 days.

Pico de Gallo

Cookbook author and cooking school teacher extraordinaire Jane Butel inspired this salsa. Her cookbook Jane Butel's Southwestern Kitchen *is my favorite source for a multitude of southwestern dishes. This smoky, fiery salsa is the traditional accompaniment for fajitas. From the Spanish "beak of the rooster," this zippy salsa will have you crowing like a rooster from the first bite.*

Makes approximately 1-1/2 cups

3 large chipotle chiles, softened in 1/4 cup hot water and chopped, water reserved

1 medium onion, finely chopped

1 large Roma tomato, chopped

2 garlic cloves, minced

3 tablespoons roughly chopped fresh cilantro

1/2 teaspoon kosher salt

2 tablespoons freshly squeezed lime juice

2 tablespoons red wine vinegar

1. Place all of the ingredients in a medium glass bowl. Mix well to combine. Add a small splash of the reserved chipotle water and let salsa marinate for 1 hour to allow flavors to blend. Refrigerate and serve chilled.

Chef Chat—
Chipotles are ripened, smoked, and dried jalapeños. You may also find chipotles en adobo in the Mexican ingredient aisle of your supermarket. The dried chiles are placed in tomato paste and canned. The chiles soften and flavor the tomato paste as well. To use the canned variety, take three chipotles and scrape off as much of the paste as possible, and then chop chiles. Add to salsa. Be careful: canned chipotles tend to be hotter than the dried.

Grilled Corn and Pinto Bean Salsa

The more salsas at a party, the more fun guests will have topping their fajitas. Roast the corn when the grill is hot and enjoy this classic salsa.

Makes about 4 cups

2 ears of corn

4 Roma tomatoes, seeded and finely chopped

1 medium red onion, finely diced

2 jalapeños, seeded and minced

1 (15-ounce) can pinto beans, drained

1/2 teaspoon toasted and ground cumin seed

1/4 cup chopped cilantro

Juice of 1 lime

Salt and pepper, to taste

1. Husk corn and grill over high heat until kernels are nicely browned. Cut kernels off cob and place in a medium bowl.

2. Add tomatoes, onion, jalapeños, pinto beans, cumin, cilantro, and lime juice; stir to combine.

3. Season with salt and pepper and allow salsa to sit for 30 minutes before serving.

above: Salsa stuff

Lime Chicken Fajitas

Lime juice tenderizes the chicken, and all that garlic really gives this dish some zip. The use of a meat tenderizer ensures that the flavors of the garlic and lime permeate the chicken and tenderize it. To prevent your fajita meat from drying out on the grill, always grill it in whole pieces and then slice it.

Serves 8

3 pounds boneless, skinless chicken breasts

6 garlic cloves, chopped

Juice of 3 limes

1 teaspoon kosher salt

1 teaspoon freshly ground pepper

1. Rinse the chicken under cold water and dry with paper towels. Trim the breasts of all fat and connective tissue. Use a meat tenderizer to make small holes in the chicken flesh.

2. In a small bowl combine garlic and lime juice. Season breasts with salt and pepper and place in a large shallow glass or porcelain dish. Pour garlic-lime mixture over chicken; turn breasts once to cover both sides of meat with marinade. Cover with plastic wrap and refrigerate for 1 hour prior to grilling.

3. Prepare the grill. Drain the breasts and place over hot heat source. Grill chicken 4 minutes on each side or until meat is cooked completely through. Remove from heat and slice in 1/2-inch slices across the grain of the meat. Chicken may be held in a 150-degree-F oven, covered with aluminum foil, for up to 1 hour. Serve hot with Fajita Fixin's (see page 153).

Jerked Pork Fajitas

Though certainly not a traditional southwestern flavor, the chile kick this Jamaican-inspired marinade gets from the habanero chiles makes it a perfect addition to the fajita grill.

Serves 8

3 pounds lean boneless pork chops

Jerk Marinade (for 3 pounds of pork)

2 habanero chiles or 3 or more jalapeños, seeded and finely chopped

2 teaspoons ground allspice

1/2 teaspoon cinnamon

1 teaspoon nutmeg

2 tablespoons kosher salt

1 tablespoon molasses

2 tablespoons apple cider vinegar

2 tablespoons lime juice

1/2 red onion, diced

Zest of 2 oranges

1 teaspoon lime zest

2 teaspoons tamarind paste, available at Asian markets

1. Place all marinade ingredients in a food processor and blend until smooth. Be very careful when working with habanero chiles—the juice can burn your skin. Wear rubber gloves when cutting them.

2. Trim any fat from pork chops and tenderize with meat tenderizing tool. Carefully spread a thin layer of the Jerk Marinade onto both sides of pork, cover, and refrigerate for 1 hour.

3. Prepare the grill and remove the pork from the marinade. Grill for 4 minutes on each side or until meat is completely cooked through. Lean pork chops cook quickly and should reach an internal temperature of 155 degrees F. If you do not have an instant-read meat thermometer, cut a slice of the chop and see if it is cooked through but still has a hint of pink in the center.

4. Slice pork across the grain and serve with Fajita Fixin's (see page 153).

Cilantro-Grilled Flank Steak Fajitas

This marinade works great on any steak before grilling. For fajitas, use the tasty flank cut.

Serves 6 to 8

1 (3-pound) flank steak
Juice of 2 limes
3 garlic cloves, minced
1/4 cup roughly chopped fresh cilantro
2 teaspoons kosher salt
2 teaspoons freshly ground pepper

1. Tenderize steaks with meat tenderizer. Mix together lime juice, garlic, and cilantro in a small bowl.
2. Season steak on both sides with salt and pepper. Place in a shallow glass or porcelain pan and pour lime-cilantro mixture over steaks. Turn flank once to cover both sides with marinade.
3. Cover with plastic wrap and place in refrigerator. Marinate for 1 hour before grilling.
4. Remove meat from marinade and grill it over hot coals or preheated gas grill until desired doneness is reached. Slice the flank across the grain in 1/2-inch slices and serve with Fajita Fixin's (see page 153).

Fajita Fixin's

I think it's much more interesting to offer a variety of grilled meats on your fajita platter. You should plan on 3 ounces of each meat per person if you are offering three choices (such as chicken, beef, and pork), or 4 ounces of each meat per person if you are offering two choices. If vegetarians are in the group, I include grilled zucchini and yellow squash on the pepper and onion plate to fill out their fajitas. Pick up a variety of ethnic hot sauces and surround your fajita platter with the colorful bottles.

Serves 8

2 cups seared red bell pepper strips*

2 cups seared yellow bell pepper strips*

2 cups seared red onion slices*

16 grilled scallions, 1 inch of tops and root ends removed

16 Homemade Flour Tortillas, warmed briefly on the grill (see page 145)

1/2 cup fresh cilantro leaves

2 cups Great Guacamole (see page 146)

1 cup Pico de Gallo (see page 147)

1 cup Grilled Corn and Pinto Bean Salsa (see page 148)

1 cup sour cream

3 limes, cut into wedges

Assorted hot sauces

2 cups grated sharp Cheddar cheese

1. Cut up peppers and onions and have them ready to sizzle in the skillet. Send the scallions and tortillas out to the grill meister with directions to pop them on the grill just before your guests are ready to assemble around the buffet.

2. Heat up a large frying pan until very hot and toss sliced peppers and onions into the pan. Stirring constantly, allow the veggies to brown by keeping them moving in the hot pan. Remove from pan and sprinkle with a few pinches of kosher salt.

3. Sear the peppers and onions as you are slicing the meat. Top the grilled meat platter with the grilled scallions and some fresh cilantro.

*Restaurant fajitas are always served with peppers and onions swimming in oil and sizzling on the platter. The extra oil coats your tongue and prevents you from enjoying the natural sweet flavor of the peppers and onions. Serve on the platter with the grilled meats.

facing: Seared scallions

Chocolate Pine Nut Tacos

Serves 6

6 taco shells

3 cups vanilla ice cream, softened slightly, divided

1 cup chocolate chips

3/4 cup toasted pine nuts

1/3 cup chocolate syrup

Powdered sugar

1. Carefully fill each taco shell with 1/2 cup ice cream and place in freezer.
2. Place chocolate chips in a small metal bowl set over simmering water. Allow chips to melt completely and remove from heat.
3. Put pine nuts in a shallow medium bowl. Dip the edges of each taco shell into the chocolate and then dip immediately into the pine nuts. Return to the freezer until ice cream is firm. At this stage you can place each taco in a small plastic bag and store for up to 1 week.
4. To serve, drizzle chocolate syrup in a swirl design on each serving plate. Place taco on plate, drizzle with more syrup, and dust with light sprinkling of powdered sugar. Serve immediately.

Chef Chat—

Experiment with different flavors of your favorite ice cream, or try combining sorbets and ice creams. The nuts you use can be exchanged for peanuts, pistachios, pecans, and so on. Kids love making these tacos. Buy extra taco shells in case they arrive broken or break as you are filling them. To refresh the crispness of store-bought taco shells, bake in a 300-degree-F oven for 5 minutes. Allow them to cool completely before filling with ice cream.

above: Chocolate dip

facing: Lindsay loves this dreamy dessert

sauce on the side

WE'VE GOT YOU COVERED

— Menu —

• Classic Hollandaise Sauce • Béchamel Sauce •

• Beurre Blanc • Mayonnaise Variations •

• Parmesan Rind Tomato Sauce •

• A Great Red Sauce • Hot-and-Sour Sauce •

• Red Chile Sauce • Chimichurri Sauce •

• Quick Bordelaise Sauce •

• Chicken Marsala • Crème Anglaise •

What makes food in restaurants taste different than the food we cook at home is the sauces that a chef creates to give his or her food that *je ne sais quoi*—that little extra something. I grew up in an era when sauces started with some kind of Campbell's soup from the can.

Just look at those old church and ladies' club cookbooks circa 1960s and you will find a multitude of recipes where a meat is placed in a casserole dish over a bed of rice or potatoes and covered with cream of chicken, mushroom, or celery soup. A Vollertsen family favorite still to this day is chicken breasts covered with cream of chicken soup stirred together with sour cream, a can of water, and then topped with frozen tater tots and baked until bubbling and golden brown. Talk about saturated fats and sodium!

We have come some way since the dark ages of American cookery, thanks partially to Julia Child and FoodTV. Our "Sauce on the Side" class at Las Cosas Cooking School always sells out, which encourages me to believe that the home cooks of today yearn to have their cooking taste world class.

facing: Steamed and sauced

Sauces can be grouped into three categories: stable, semi-stable and a-la-minute. Stable sauces such as red chile sauce, caramel sauce, mayonnaise, and the hot-and-sour sauce are completely emulsified and will not separate or "break" when held for long periods of time.

Semi-stable sauces like hollandaise and Beurre Blanc can be held at a very low temperature for several hours but cannot be chilled and rewarmed, as the fat and liquid elements will separate.

A-la-minute sauces such as piccata and marsala are made in the pan as the dish is being created. Practice the skill of sauce preparation and your dishes will come alive with the addition of one of these classic sauces.

above: A slow butter drizzle

Classic Hollandaise Sauce

This sauce, served over blanched asparagus or poached eggs, or transformed into béarnaise with the addition of chopped tarragon, is certainly the richest of all mother sauces.

Makes about 2 cups

1/3 cup water
1/3 cup freshly squeezed lemon juice
1/2 teaspoon salt
1/4 teaspoon white pepper
3 large egg yolks
16 tablespoons unsalted butter, melted and clarified*
1 tablespoon white wine vinegar

1. Combine water, lemon juice, salt, and pepper in a small saucepan over medium heat; allow it to reduce until there are 2 tablespoons liquid remaining. Remove from heat and cool.
2. Place egg yolks in a medium metal bowl and whisk in lemon reduction. Place bowl over a saucepan of simmering water and whisk until mixture thickens. Take bowl off the heat and slowly drizzle in clarified butter and vinegar, alternating drops of each and whisking continuously.
3. Hold hollandaise at 150 degrees F until use. (A small thermos is perfect for keeping sauce warm.)

To clarify butter, place butter in a small saucepan and set over low heat. Allow butter to melt completely and then carefully skim milky foam off the surface using a small ladle or spoon. Avoid the milky water left in the bottom of the pan when whisking into hollandaise.

Chef Chat—
Whisking and pouring at the same time is a bit tricky if you are working alone. To prevent the bowl from spinning as you whisk in the butter and vinegar, wet a large tea towel and wrap it in a circle the same circumference of your bowl. Place the bowl on the towel and nestle it down so that it will not move as you whisk.

A Great Red Sauce

I did a class for a group of young mothers who wanted a menu of quick, easy, and versatile recipes. This simple tomato sauce can also be transformed into yummy soup!

Serves 6

2 tablespoons olive oil

2 garlic cloves, minced

1/4 cup minced onion

2 (14.5-ounce) cans diced tomatoes

1/2 cup dry white wine

8 fresh basil leaves, roughly chopped

Salt and pepper, to taste

1. Place olive oil in a medium soup pot and heat pan over medium heat. Add garlic and onions, and sauté until onions become translucent. Add canned tomatoes and sauté for 5 minutes.

2. Add wine and cook over medium heat for 10 minutes. Stir in fresh basil and season with salt and pepper. Serve as a pasta sauce.

Variation for Tomato Soup:

Add 4 cups vegetable stock

1. Purée soup carefully and serve hot, garnished with croutons and grated Parmigiano-Reggiano cheese.

facing: Fettuccine with Red Sauce

Hot-and-Sour Sauce

I love to introduce students to the flavorful ingredients of Asian cooking. This recipe is a fabulous coming together of sweet, hot, salty, and sour.

Makes 2 cups

1 lemongrass stalk, bottom 2/3 only, thinly sliced

1/4 cup peeled and finely sliced fresh ginger

2 star anise

3 cups chicken stock

2 teaspoons peanut oil

1 cup thinly sliced shiitake mushrooms

1/2 cup finely chopped onion

1 teaspoon minced garlic

2 Thai chiles, seeded and sliced

2 teaspoons Thai fish sauce

1/3 cup rice vinegar

1/2 teaspoon white pepper

1 teaspoon sugar

2 tablespoons cold water

2 teaspoons rice flour or cornstarch

1/4 cup fresh whole basil leaves

Salt, to taste

1/4 cup chopped scallions, root ends discarded

Chef Chat—
Serve this delicious sauce over steamed or sautéed fish, shrimp, or chicken with lots of jasmine rice.

1. Place lemongrass, ginger, star anise, and stock in a medium saucepan, and simmer until reduced by half.
2. Meanwhile, place oil in skillet and sauté mushrooms, onion, garlic, and chiles over medium heat until mushrooms are soft.
3. Strain stock and add to mushroom mixture. Add fish sauce, rice vinegar, pepper, and sugar, and mix well.
4. In a small bowl combine cold water and rice flour; stir until smooth to form a "slurry."
5. Whisk rice flour slurry into sauce, add basil, and simmer just until slightly thickened. Adjust seasoning.
6. Keep warm until ready to use; scatter chopped scallions over sauce before serving.

Red Chile Sauce

If New Mexico had a mother sauce, this would be it. Every single version you will taste in our food-fabulous state will be slightly different. It's used to create enchiladas, top tamales and burgers, and nestle under chile rellenos.

Makes approximately 2-3/4 cups

1 tablespoon butter
1 tablespoon flour
1/4 cup mild ground red chile
1 tablespoon ancho chile powder
1/4 cup ground hot red chile
2 garlic cloves, minced
1/2 teaspoon dried Mexican oregano
1/2 teaspoon ground cumin
2-3/4 cups stock (vegetable, chicken, or beef)
1 teaspoon salt

1. Melt butter in a heavy saucepan over medium-low heat. Whisk in flour and cook until roux turns golden yellow, about 5 minutes.
2. Remove from heat and stir in ground chiles. Return pan to heat and whisk in garlic, oregano, cumin, and stock. Reduce heat to low.
3. Allow sauce to simmer for 10 minutes and season with salt.

Chef Chat—
The dish you are making will determine which stock is best to use for the sauce. For general use, I prefer chicken stock, but for rellenos I use vegetable stock, as rellenos can be a yummy vegetarian dish. If you are making beef enchiladas, use beef stock for the sauce, and so on. If you find this sauce too spicy, simply increase the amount of mild ground chile and decrease the amount of hot you use in the recipe. Many restaurants still make their chile sauce using dried chiles. Using the pure ground chile powders saves the steps of puréeing and straining the sauce. Chile sauce freezes well.

Crème Anglaise

Pour this delicious vanilla sauce over apple crumbles, fruit crisps, and bread puddings—anywhere a sweet, creamy sauce will taste at home.

Makes about 2 cups

1-1/2 cups milk

1 cup heavy cream

1 teaspoon vanilla

1/3 cup sugar

2 tablespoons cornstarch

3 egg yolks

1. Place the milk, cream, and vanilla in a saucepan and bring to a boil. Remove from heat, cover, and keep hot.
2. Whisk together sugar and cornstarch in a medium bowl. Add egg yolks and whisk until the mixture whitens and forms a ribbon.
3. Pour warm milk over egg mixture, whisking constantly.
4. Return mixture to pan and slowly return to a boil, stirring constantly. Remove from heat. Allow custard to cool and adjust thickness by adding more milk.

Chef Chat—
For a delicious topping for apple or peach pie, add 1/4 teaspoon nutmeg, 1/8 teaspoon ground cloves, and a pinch ground cardamom to the sauce at the very end to create a Spiced Crème Anglaise.

facing: White Chocolate Cranberry Bread Pudding with Crème Anglaise

hostess with the mostest

— Menu —

- Cumin Toasted Almonds -
- Charred Red Peppers with Herbed Goat Cheese -
- Smoky Baba Ghanoush - Crostini Pomodoro -
- Apple and Chicken Liver Pâté - Charleston Crab Cakes -
- Smoked Potatoes with Balsamic Syrup and Gorgonzola -
- Flourless Chocolate Torte - Lemon Curd -

Many of our students are busy moms and dads who would like to learn how to simplify entertaining and throw a great party without losing their minds. I always recommend to my wannabe caterers to think about buying some of the goodies you will serve from one of the great gourmet food stores in your town.

The obvious items your guests won't mind in a store-bought version are olives, cheeses, pâtés, artisan breads and bread sticks, and spreads like hummus, baba ghanoush, and the like.

Build your menu around a favorite family recipe or sumptuous homemade dessert and shortcut the rest of the preparations. Always try new recipes before the night of the party to work out kinks and tackle cooking pratfalls. Nothing is more terrifying than having guests at the door and you're not done with cooking and cleanup.

Don't forget to offer vegetarian options as part of your menu; there are more out there than you think. Also, having a variety of interesting nonalcoholic drinks on hand shows your guests they don't have to get hammered.

Think about hiring a waiter, bartender, or cleanup person to allow you to enjoy your own party and not go to bed with a huge mess to face in the morning. If a recipe fails, change the name of the dish and serve it anyway! -

facing: Hostess Lindsay serves Charred Red Peppers with Herbed Goat Cheese

Cumin Toasted Almonds

These zippy nuts take only minutes to make.

Serves 4

1 tablespoon toasted and ground cumin seeds

1/4 teaspoon toasted and ground coriander seeds

1/4 teaspoon red pepper flakes

1 teaspoon kosher salt

2 tablespoons extra virgin olive oil

8 ounces whole, unblanched almonds

1. Heat the oven to 400 degrees F. In a large, shallow bowl, combine cumin, coriander, pepper flakes, salt, and oil. Set aside.

2. Place the almonds in a single layer on a baking sheet. Place the baking sheet in the center of the oven and toast until the nuts are lightly browned, fragrant, and making crackling sounds, about 8 minutes.

3. Remove baking sheet from the oven. Immediately add the hot nuts to the spice mixture. Stir for at least 1 minute to coat the almonds evenly and thoroughly. Taste and adjust for seasoning. Serve warm or at room temperature. The almonds can be stored, well-sealed, for up to 2 weeks. To refresh, reheat in a hot oven.

Charred Red Peppers with Herbed Goat Cheese

These pretty pinwheels are quick and easy to make and are loaded with the flavors of summer—herbs and creamy goat cheese.

Serves 6

2 large red bell peppers

8 ounces goat cheese

1/4 cup chopped assorted fresh herbs (basil, thyme, oregano, chives)

1 shallot, minced

1/2 teaspoon salt

1/2 teaspoon pepper

Juice of 1/2 lemon

Extra virgin olive oil to drizzle

1 lemon, cut in wedges

1. Roast peppers over direct heat to char the skin. Place in paper bag and allow to cool.
2. Mix goat cheese, herbs, shallot, salt, pepper, and lemon juice in a small bowl.
3. Peel, seed, and devein roasted peppers and lay flat.
4. Divide goat cheese between the peppers and fill pepper cavity.
5. Roll peppers up, wrap tightly in plastic wrap, and allow to chill for 1 hour.
6. Slice peppers in a pinwheel fashion and place on platter.
7. Drizzle with olive oil and serve with lemon wedges.

Smoky Baba Ghanoush

By roasting the eggplant directly over the flame, the most wonderful smoky flavor is added to this already scrumptious dip.

Serves 4 to 6

1 (2-pound) eggplant

3 garlic cloves, or to taste

1/3 cup tahini (sesame paste)

Juice of 2 lemons, or more to taste

1/4 cup whole-milk yogurt

1/4 teaspoon red pepper flakes

Kosher salt, to taste

Drizzle of extra virgin olive oil

1 tablespoon chopped parsley

1. Wash the eggplant, prick it all over with a fork, and place directly over the high flame of a gas stove or outdoor grill. Turn the eggplant occasionally and let it blacken, become soft, and start to collapse. Alternatively, place the eggplant in a roasting dish and roast in a preheated 500-degree-F oven, allowing it to bake until it collapses.

2. Allow the eggplant to cool. Peel it and chop the flesh. Place in a colander. Set over a plate and allow to drain for 15 minutes.

3. Place eggplant flesh in a food processor fitted with a steel blade and add the garlic, tahini, lemon juice, and yogurt. Purée until smooth. Season with red pepper flakes and salt. Add additional lemon juice if necessary.

4. Place in a serving bowl and drizzle with olive oil. Top with parsley. Serve with Rosemary Flatbread (see page 39) or toasted pita breads.

above: Charring the eggplant

Crostini Pomodoro

Serves 6 to 8

8 Roma tomatoes

3 tablespoons olive oil, divided

2 garlic cloves, minced

8 large basil leaves, sliced chiffonade

1 teaspoon kosher salt

Freshly ground pepper

Splash balsamic vinegar

1 baguette

1. Stand each tomato on its stem end and slice off the flesh, in 3 to 4 slices, leaving as much of the seeds on the core as possible. Slice each piece into thin strips and then cut across strips into a fine dice.
2. Place tomatoes in a medium bowl and add 2 tablespoons olive oil, garlic, basil, salt, pepper, and vinegar. Stir together and set aside.
3. Slice baguette on the diagonal into 1/4-inch slices. Brush each slice lightly with remaining olive oil and bake in a preheated 400-degree-F oven until nicely browned, about 8 minutes.
4. Allow crostini to cool and then top each with a teaspoon of tomato salsa.

above: *Tasty tomato topping*

Apple and Chicken Liver Pâté

I am surprised how many people actually love chicken liver pâté. The hint of apple adds sweetness and cuts the fat. It's very cost-effective for a large party. Remember, it is rich, so a little goes a long way.

Serves 8 to 9

8 ounces chicken livers, cleaned and rinsed (look for organic)

2 teaspoons flour

3 teaspoons unsalted butter

Handful fresh sage leaves

3 shallots, minced

1 garlic clove, minced

1/2 Granny Smith apple, peeled, cored, and sliced

1 tablespoon brandy

Salt and pepper, to taste

1. Pat chicken livers dry with paper towels. Dust with flour.
2. Melt butter in medium skillet and quick-fry the sage leaves. Remove leaves with slotted spoon, drain on paper towel, and set aside.
3. Add shallots and garlic to pan, and sauté until soft but not browned. Add apple and cook until tender.
4. Add chicken livers and sauté until medium-rare. Flame with brandy.
5. Transfer liver mixture into a food processor work bowl fitted with a steel blade and purée until smooth.
6. Season with salt and pepper and turn pâté into a bowl. Cover with plastic wrap and chill until service.
7. To serve, spread pâté on toasted baguette slices and top with reserved sage leaves.

Charleston Crab Cakes

Everyone loves crab cakes, and bite-size versions are perfect to serve as an hors d'oeuvre. The remoulade sauce described on page 162 makes a perfect accompanying dip.

Serves 6

3 tablespoons olive oil

1/4 cup finely chopped red bell pepper

1/4 cup finely chopped celery

1/4 cup finely chopped onion

1 pound fresh crabmeat, picked through

1/4 cup minced fresh dill

2 tablespoons Dijon mustard

1/4 teaspoon nutmeg

1/2 teaspoon smoked Spanish paprika

1/4 teaspoon freshly ground pepper

1/4 teaspoon celery salt

1/4 teaspoon cayenne pepper

1 cup fresh breadcrumbs

3 egg whites

1/2 cup vegetable oil for sautéing

1 lemon, cut into 6 wedges

1. Heat olive oil in a large skillet over medium heat. Add bell pepper, celery, and onion, and sauté until they soften, 4 to 5 minutes. Do not let vegetables brown.

2. Transfer the vegetables to a large mixing bowl and cool slightly. Add the crabmeat, dill, mustard, spices, and breadcrumbs. Beat egg whites until frothy and add to the bowl. Mix ingredients together; the mixture should be moist enough to stick together.

3. Dip your hands in cold water, and then form 1-inch crab cakes using about 1 heaping tablespoon of the mixture. Then flatten and round each cake so it is 1 inch thick.

4. Heat vegetable oil in a skillet over medium heat. Place crab cakes, a few at a time, in the pan and cook until golden brown, 2 to 3 minutes. Gently turn cakes over and cook other side 2 to 3 minutes.

5. Preheat oven to 350 degrees F. Place browned crab cakes on a baking sheet and heat through until they are hot in the middle. Serve with lemon wedges and/or tartare sauce.

Apple Cinnamon Fritters

I occasionally do a class called "Wonders with Wontons" that demonstrates the versatility of this readily available Asian ingredient. This is an apple-licious dessert I created for that class.

Makes about 40 fritters, serves 8

3 Granny Smith apples, peeled, cored, and
    finely chopped
1 tablespoon sugar
1/4 teaspoon cinnamon
1/4 teaspoon nutmeg

1/2 teaspoon fresh lemon juice
1/4 cup raisins or dried cranberries
1 package wonton wrappers
4 cups vegetable oil
Powdered sugar

1. Toss apples in sugar, cinnamon, nutmeg, and lemon juice. Add raisins and allow to marinate for 10 minutes.
2. Take 1/2 teaspoon of filling and place on the middle of wonton wrapper. With a wet finger, dampen perimeter of wrapper and fold over; crimp to seal fritter.
3. Heat oil to 350 degrees F and fry fritters in batches of 6 until crispy and golden brown. Drain on paper towels and dust with powdered sugar.
4. Serve warm, drizzled with Caramel Sauce.

Caramel Sauce

1/4 cup water
1 cup sugar
1 cup heavy cream
Pinch salt

Chef Chat—
Use a squeeze bottle to drizzle the sauce on these yummy fritters. Wonton wrappers are wonderful things; they can be filled with a variety of stuffings and then boiled, steamed, or fried. Use them in place of pasta dough for ravioli if you don't have a pasta machine.

1. Place water and sugar in a heavy-bottomed saucepan. (DO NOT use a nonstick pan.)
2. Bring sugar syrup to a boil and allow to cook until mixture reaches a deep golden brown color, about 10 minutes. Use a pastry brush dipped in cold water to keep the sides of the pan free of crystallized sugar.
3. Carefully add heavy cream and continue to stir until sugar lumps completely dissolve, about 10 minutes.
4. Remove from heat and stir in salt. Sauce may be reheated in the microwave.

Spa Chocolate Sorbet

One of my favorite part-time jobs was chef-ing at a spa close to Santa Fe called Vista Clara Ranch. This decadent fat-free sorbet helped the guests feel spoiled, and it satisfies even the most intense chocolate craving.

Makes 1-1/2 quarts

1-1/4 cups sugar
1-1/4 cups cocoa
1-1/4 cups hot decaf coffee
1-1/4 cups boiling water
2 tablespoons Kahlúa (coffee-flavored liqueur)
Pinch salt

1. Whisk together sugar and cocoa in a medium bowl. Pour coffee and boiling water over sugar-cocoa mixture, and stir until sugar is completely dissolved. Allow to cool completely.

2. Stir in Kahlúa and salt. Freeze in an ice cream freezer according to manufacturer's instructions. Alternatively, pour mixture into large rectangular glass or ceramic container and freeze until slushy. Take out of freezer and scrape surface of sorbet; return to freezer. Do this twice more and then allow to freeze completely. This will create a more granite-like sorbet. Store in a covered plastic container.

Grilled Pears with Fennel Syrup and Mascarpone

When the heat hits, consider preparing even the dessert outside on the grill.

Serves 6

6 Bosc or other firm pears
1/4 cup butter, melted
3/4 cup water
3/4 cup sugar
1/3 cup crushed fennel seeds
8 ounces mascarpone cheese
Mint leaves for garnish

1. Peel pears; halve and core them. Prepare grill and brush pears with melted butter. Grill pears until they are nicely browned but still firm. Remove from grill and leave at room temperature.
2. Make the fennel syrup by placing water, sugar, and fennel seeds in a medium saucepan. Bring to a boil and then reduce heat to a simmer. Allow syrup to cook until it thickens slightly, about 20 minutes. Strain out fennel seeds.
3. Make a heaping scoop of the mascarpone with a melon baller or small ice cream scoop and place in each cored pear. Place two halves on each of 6 serving plates. Drizzle pears with fennel syrup and garnish with mint leaves.

above: Peel, grill, stuff

Guava Cake

Most Central and South American countries have a version of this pastry, called Pastel de Guayaba, that celebrates tart guavas.

Serves 8

3/4 cup butter

1 cup sugar

2 eggs

1 teaspoon vanilla

1 teaspoon lemon zest

2 cups plus 2 tablespoons flour

1 teaspoon baking powder

1/4 teaspoon salt

10.5 ounces guava paste (half of a 21-ounce can)

1. Preheat oven to 375 degrees F. Cream the butter and sugar together in a medium bowl until light and fluffy.
2. Add the eggs, 1 at a time, beating after each addition.
3. Add vanilla and lemon zest. Sift together flour, baking powder, and salt into a medium bowl. Add to egg batter and beat until well combined.
4. Spread half of the batter into an 8 x 8-inch baking pan. Slice guava paste into 1/4-inch slices and layer over batter. Spread the rest of the batter over the guava slices.
5. Bake for 45 minutes or until a toothpick inserted into the center comes out clean. Allow to cool and sprinkle with powdered sugar.

Chef Chat—
Look for guava paste in the Mexican section of your grocery store. It comes in round tins and Goya makes a popular brand. This is more like a guava-filled shortbread cookie or "Guava Newton," if you will.

Spiced Fruit Cobbler

This quick dessert will show off any fruit you use.

Serves 6 to 8

6 cups sliced fresh or frozen fruit

3/4 cup sugar, divided

1/2 cup flour

1 teaspoon baking powder

Pinch salt

1/4 teaspoon nutmeg

1/8 teaspoon ground cloves

Pinch ground cardamom

8 tablespoons cold unsalted butter, cut into bits

1 egg, beaten

1/2 teaspoon vanilla

1. Preheat oven to 400 degrees F. Toss fruit in 1/4 cup sugar and scatter into a lightly buttered 9-inch round baking pan.

2. In a food processor fitted with a steel blade, combine flour, baking powder, salt, remaining sugar, nutmeg, cloves, and cardamom, and pulse once or twice to mix.

3. Add butter and process for 10 seconds, until mixture is well mixed.

4. Place mixture in a medium bowl and stir in egg and vanilla.

5. Drop mixture onto fruit by tablespoonfuls, but do not spread batter out. Bake until golden brown, 30 to 35 minutes. Serve warm with ice cream or Crème Anglaise (see page 171).

White Chocolate Cranberry Bread Pudding

I never liked raisins as a kid, perhaps because someone told me they were bugs in a cookie. That's why I was thrilled to find this recipe offered by a guest chef: bread pudding sans raisins.

Serves 8 to 10

3 cups heavy cream

1 cup milk

8 eggs

1 cup sugar

1 teaspoon vanilla

6 cups diced white bread

1/2 cup dried cranberries

4 ounces white chocolate, cut into small chunks

1. Mix together cream, milk, eggs, sugar, and vanilla in a large bowl. Add bread, cranberries, and white chocolate, and let soak for 20 minutes.

2. Butter a 9 x 13 x 2-inch casserole. Add bread mixture and bake at 375 degrees F for 1 hour, or until custard is set. Serve either chilled or warm, dusted lightly with powdered sugar.

above: Dessert is served

Zabaglione with Berries

Zabaglione is traditionally served warm. This version is chilled and can be made well in advance.

Serves 6

5 egg yolks

3/4 cup powdered sugar

6 tablespoons sweet Marsala

2 cups heavy cream

3 cups fresh berries (raspberries, strawberries, blackberries)

Fresh mint sprigs

1. Combine yolks, sugar, and Marsala in metal mixing bowl and place over simmering pan of water, making sure the bottom of the bowl is not touching the water.
2. Whisk mixture until it has thickened and is fluffy and golden yellow. Remove from heat and allow to cool.
3. Whip cream to soft peaks.
4. Gently fold cream into zabaglione and refrigerate for 1 hour, until set.
5. Serve with fresh fruit on chilled plates and garnish with mint.

Chocolate Nutella Torte

This torte is very rich; a sliver is all you need. It freezes well when wrapped tightly in foil and then plastic. Nutella outsells peanut butter in Europe and is widely available here. Refrigerate after opening if you can resist finishing the jar.

Serves 12

9 ounces bittersweet chocolate, chopped*

1/2 cup unsalted butter

1/2 cup sugar

1/2 cup Nutella

3 tablespoons Frangelico hazelnut liquor

5 large eggs

1 tablespoon cocoa

1. In a medium metal bowl sitting over simmering water, melt chocolate, butter, sugar, and Nutella, stirring until smooth. Remove from heat and allow to cool slightly. Stir in Frangelico.
2. In a large bowl, whisk eggs until well mixed; add cocoa and completely incorporate. Whisk chocolate mixture into eggs and mix well.
3. Generously grease a 9-inch springform pan. Line the bottom of the pan with parchment paper and grease the paper.
4. Tightly wrap outside of pan with aluminum foil. Pour batter into pan and place pan into a large roasting pan.
5. Add hot water to the roasting pan until water is halfway up the side of springform pan.
6. Bake at 350 degrees F for 35 minutes or until the edge of cake is set. Center of cake will still be slightly soft.
7. Remove pan sides and cool on rack 30 minutes.
8. Flip cake onto serving platter so that the bottom is now the top and carefully remove parchment paper. Chill or serve at room temperature.

* *Gadget Gab—Use a chocolate and ice rake to save breaking off the tip of your favorite knife.*

a Dickens christmas feast

BRITISH AND BOUNTIFUL

– Menu –

· Cheddar and Ale Soup ·

· Pub-Style Scotch Eggs ·

· Warm Salad of Wilted Spinach, Apples, and Stilton ·

· Roast Goose with Chestnut-Caramelized Pear Stuffing and Braised Red Cabbage ·

· Festive Sherry Trifle ·

· Sticky Date Pudding ·

My college had an exchange program that sent students to Leeds, England, to spend a semester studying hospitality at Leeds Polytechnic. It was an exciting trip for me, and an eye-opener to experience food outside of the Campbell's Soup realm of my youth in Rochester, New York. Leeds is located in Yorkshire, land of puddings, blood sausages, and bubble and squeak. The fog and drizzle of the holiday season had you craving rich and slow-cooked foods. What better time of year than Christmas to honor our forefathers and re-create a menu from Olde England. ·

facing: Festive Santa Fe wreath

Cheddar and Ale Soup

I love this soup. The slight crunch the celery and onions give it are a great counterpoint texture to the smooth and creamy combo of Cheddar and cream.

Serves 6 to 8

3 tablespoons butter

1 cup chopped onion

1/2 cup minced celery

2 cloves garlic, minced

1 teaspoon toasted and ground caraway seeds

3 tablespoons flour

1 cup English ale

3 cups chicken stock

2 cups grated sharp Cheddar cheese

1 cup heavy cream

Salt and pepper, to taste

2 tablespoons chopped chives for garnish

1. Melt butter in a medium heavy-bottomed soup pot and sauté onions and celery for 5 minutes over medium heat. Add garlic and caraway seeds and sauté for 2 minutes more.

2. Sprinkle flour over onion mixture and mix well, cooking for an additional 3 minutes.

3. Add ale, including the foam, and deglaze pan thoroughly. Stir in the stock and the cheese, and mix until the cheese has melted. Turn the heat to low and simmer for 15 minutes, stirring occasionally.

4. Just before serving, gently stir in cream and season with salt and pepper. Garnish with chopped chives.

above: Santa Fe snow

Pub-Style Scotch Eggs

What a delicious and very British twist on sausage and eggs. Served warm in pubs, Scotch Eggs make a great lunch or late-night snack, especially satisfying after a few pints of ale.

Serves 4

1 1/4 pounds bulk country-style sausage,
    such as Jimmy Dean, uncooked
1/2 teaspoon dried thyme
1 teaspoon crumbled dried sage
Pinch cayenne pepper
1 tablespoon chopped parsley
4 hard-boiled eggs, peeled
2 large eggs, beaten
1/2 cup flour
1 cup fresh breadcrumbs
Vegetable oil for frying

1. Mix together sausage, spices, and herbs in a large bowl and divide into 4 equal portions. Place each portion on a piece of wax paper and flatten it into a thin circle, 1/8 inch thick.

2. Set hard-boiled egg in center of sausage and enclose it completely. Pat sausage into place. Wet hands to prevent sausage from sticking to you.

3. Place beaten eggs in a shallow bowl, flour in a second bowl, and breadcrumbs in a third.

4. Heat 2 1/2 inches vegetable oil in a large skillet and bring it to 350 degrees F. Dredge the sausage-coated eggs in the flour, then into the beaten egg, and finally into the breadcrumbs.

5. Fry eggs 2 at a time in the heated oil, turning occasionally, until golden brown. Check to make sure sausage is cooked through. If eggs start to brown too quickly before sausage is cooked, you may finish them in a 350-degree-F oven for 10 minutes or so. Drain on paper towels, slice in half, and serve hot with English mustard and your favorite pickles.

Warm Salad of Wilted Spinach, Apples, and Stilton

I'll take my blue cheese any way I can. And Stilton just might be my favorite variety. You'll love the holiday colors of green and red that this salad features. It's perfect for festive entertaining.

Serves 8

1/4 cup olive oil

8 ounces slab bacon, cut into 1/2-inch pieces

2 tablespoons chopped shallots

8 cups baby spinach, washed and dried

1 tablespoon Dijon mustard

3 tablespoons sherry vinegar

1/4 cup crumbled Stilton, or to taste

2 Granny Smith apples, peeled and sliced

4 teaspoons dried cranberries

Freshly ground pepper

1. Place olive oil in a skillet and turn heat to medium. Add bacon and cook slowly until bacon becomes crisp. Remove bacon with a slotted spoon and drain on paper towels. Drain all but 3 tablespoons of fat in the skillet and return pan to heat.

2. Add the shallots and cook for 2 minutes, until shallots soften. Add bacon to the pan.

3. Place spinach in large mixing bowl. Add mustard and vinegar to the skillet and heat until bubbling.

4. Pour vinegar mixture over spinach and toss quickly.

5. Divide spinach between salad plates. Scatter Stilton over salads, arrange apples and cranberries on spinach, and top with freshly ground pepper. Serve immediately.

Roast Goose with Chestnut-Caramelized Pear Stuffing and Braised Red Cabbage

You will be surprised how much lovely goose fat will be rendered from your goose as you roast it. It's important to keep removing it from the pan. Reserve it and keep it in the fridge for use throughout the holiday season.

Serves 10 to 12

1 (10–12 pound) goose, trimmed and cleaned

Kosher salt

1/2 cup butter, melted

1 tablespoon freshly ground pepper

2 tablespoons fresh thyme

1 teaspoon toasted and ground caraway seeds

Kosher salt

2 pounds Granny Smith apples, peeled, cored, and quartered

1 cup apricots, plumped in 2 tablespoons brandy and halved

4 cups thinly sliced red cabbage

3 tablespoons cider vinegar

1. Preheat oven to 450 degrees F. Fill a large stockpot half full with cold water. Bring to a boil and gently submerge goose in water. Allow water to return to a boil and cook for 1 minute. Carefully remove goose to a large platter.

2. Meanwhile mix together butter, pepper, thyme, and caraway seeds in a small bowl.

3. Dry goose skin with paper towels. Rub goose inside and out with kosher salt.

4. Stuff goose with apples and apricots, and baste with half the butter-herb mixture.

5. Put goose on roasting rack in roasting pan and place in oven. Roast for 30 minutes.

6. Remove from oven and drain goose fat from pan using a large turkey baster. Reserve the goose fat for another use. Brush remaining butter-herb mixture onto goose. Turn oven down to 350 degrees F and return goose to oven.

7. Drain goose fat every 30 minutes and baste before returning to oven. After 2 hours, scatter red cabbage around goose in roasting pan. Sprinkle vinegar over cabbage.

8. Continue roasting goose until the juices run clear when goose is pierced in the thickest part of the thigh. Meat thermometer should reach 165 degrees F when placed into the fat part of the drumstick.

9. Allow goose to rest 20 minutes before slicing, tented loosely with foil. Serve with cabbage and apricot-apple stuffing around the roast.

Chestnut-Caramelized Pear Stuffing

Serves 8

2 tablespoons brown sugar

2 tablespoons balsamic vinegar

4 Bosc pears, cored and coarsely chopped into 1-inch pieces

3 tablespoons butter

1 cup chopped celery

1 cup chopped onions

1 loaf French baguette, torn into pieces (about 3 cups)

3 tablespoons chopped fresh sage

1 teaspoon toasted and ground caraway seeds

1 cup steamed or roasted quartered chestnuts

2 large eggs

1-1/2 cups chicken stock

1. Preheat oven to 375 degrees F. Dissolve brown sugar in balsamic vinegar. Place pears in a medium bowl and pour vinegar mixture over them. Toss pears to completely cover.

2. Drain pears and place them in a heavy-bottomed casserole dish. Bake, uncovered, for 30 minutes or until pears are nicely browned but still holding their shape.

3. Melt butter in a sauté pan and add celery and onion. Sauté over medium heat until onions brown slightly. Butter a 13 x 9 x 2-inch baking dish. Remove pears from the oven.

4. Toss bread in a large bowl and add celery and onion mix, pears, sage, caraway seeds, and chestnuts.

5. In a small bowl, whisk together eggs and stock, and stir into stuffing mix.

6. Place stuffing into baking dish and bake until cooked through and toasty, about 35 minutes.

Festive Sherry Trifle

The Brits call this "tipsy pudding" because too many servings can make you tipsy. If you are serving children this delicious dessert, you can cut way back on the amount of sherry you use or omit it altogether.

Serves 12

For the Cake:

  1 tablespoon unsalted butter

  1 cup sliced almonds

  1 teaspoon baking powder

  1/4 teaspoon salt

  6 large eggs

  1/2 cup sugar

  1 teaspoon vanilla

  1 teaspoon almond extract

1. Grease a 15 x 10 x 1-inch jellyroll pan with half the butter. Line the pan with parchment paper and grease with remaining butter. Preheat oven to 350 degrees F.
2. Place almonds in the work bowl of a food processor fitted with a steel blade and pulverize until floury looking. Add baking powder and salt.
3. Separate the eggs. In a large bowl, beat yolks and sugar with an electric mixer until thick and lemony colored. Add the vanilla and almond extracts.
4. Fold almonds into the yolk mixture and set aside.
5. With clean bowl and beaters, beat egg whites in a large bowl, until they form stiff peaks. Add a large spoonful of whites to yolk mixture and fold into mixture. Add half of remaining whites to yolks, fold in, and then add remaining whites.
6. Spread batter into pan and bake for 15 to 20 minutes until top springs back when touched. Let cake cool.*

*Or you can cheat by buying a pound cake and slicing it into finger-size slices.

continued

For the Custard:

    1 cup heavy cream

    1 cup half-and-half

    6 egg yolks

    1/4 cup sugar

    1 teaspoon vanilla

1. Meanwhile make the custard by placing cream and half-and-half in a medium saucepan. Bring to a gentle simmer over low heat. In a medium bowl, whisk yolks with sugar until lemony yellow. Whisk in the vanilla.

2. Whisk 1/4 cup of the hot cream mixture into yolks. Gradually whisk remaining cream into egg mixture. Return mixture to saucepan and cook over low heat, stirring constantly until custard is thick enough to coat the back of a wooden spoon (about 3 to 5 minutes). Cover and refrigerate until chilled.

For the Assembly:

    1 cup apricot preserves, divided

    3/4 cup dry sherry, divided

    2 cups raspberries, divided

    2 cups sliced strawberries, divided

    2 cups cream, whipped and sweetened with 1/4 cup powdered confectioners' sugar, divided

    1/2 cup toasted almond slices

    12 maraschino cherries

    Mint leaves for garnish

1. When cake is cool, slice it into 3 x 2-inch slices and set aside.

2. Spread 1/3 cup of the preserves over the bottom of a large glass bowl. Cover jam with slices of the cake and splash 3 tablespoons sherry over the cake.

3. Spread 2/3 cup of the Custard over cake and scatter 1-1/3 cups of the berries over the custard. Cover fruit with 2/3 cup of whipped cream.

4. Repeat with another layer of cake, splashed with 3 tablespoons sherry. Spread 1/3 cup jam, then 2/3 cup Custard then 1-1/3 cups berries, then cream.

5. Repeat this layering technique one more time, finishing with whipped cream.

6. Garnish with toasted almonds, and maraschino cherries. Cover with plastic wrap and chill.

7. To serve, scoop trifle onto individual plates. Garnish with fresh mint. Alternatively you can assemble the trifle in individual glasses, where only one layer of the ingredients is necessary (see photo page 206).

Layering Chart: from the bottom of the bowl

Apricot preserves
Cake
Sherry
Custard
Berries
Whipped cream
Cake
Sherry
Apricot preserves
Custard
Berries
Whipped cream
Cake
Sherry
Apricot preserves
Custard
Whipped cream
Toasted almonds
Maraschino cherries

above: Elements of trifle

Sticky Date Pudding

Years ago I did some consulting work for a high school cafeteria school lunch program. They had 1,000 pounds of government surplus dates that they couldn't get the kids to eat no matter how they served them. I gave them this recipe. I bet those kids are loving dates now!

Serves 6 to 8

For the Pudding:

1 cup chopped pitted dates

1/2 cup boiling water

2 teaspoons baking soda

1-1/4 cups sugar

1 cup unsalted butter

5 eggs

2 1/2 cups flour

1 teaspoon salt

1. Place dates in a medium bowl and pour boiling water over them. Stir in baking soda and set aside.

2. In another medium bowl, cream together sugar and butter until mixture is light and fluffy. Add the eggs, 1 at a time, beating after each addition.

3. Mix together flour and salt. Add date mixture to batter with eggs and stir to combine. Add dry ingredients and beat batter until it is well mixed.

4. Pour batter into a buttered 9 x 9 x 2-inch pan and bake in a preheated 375-degree-F oven for 25 minutes. A toothpick should come out clean when poked into center of pudding.

For the Sauce:

1 cup heavy cream

1 3/4 cups brown sugar

1/4 cup unsalted butter

1 teaspoon vanilla

1/2 teaspoon salt

1. Place cream, brown sugar, and butter in a heavy saucepan. Whisk mixture to combine and bring to a boil over medium heat. Reduce heat to low and allow sauce to simmer for 15 minutes or until it thickens.

2. Remove from heat and stir in vanilla and salt. Serve warm over Sticky Date Pudding.

index